ALLERGIC INTIMACIES

Allergic Intimacies

FOOD, DISABILITY, DESIRE, AND RISK

Michael Gill

FORDHAM UNIVERSITY PRESS   NEW YORK   2023

Visit us online at www.fordhampress.com.

Library of Congress Cataloging-in-Publication Data available online at https://catalog.loc.gov.

Printed in the United States of America

25 24 23   5 4 3 2 1

First edition

For Holly. A small dog with a big personality. You are missed.

Contents

Preface

Are food allergies disabilities? What structures and systems ensure the survival of some people with food allergies and not others? *Allergic Intimacies* is a critical engagement with food allergies in their cultural representations, advocacy, law, and stories about personal experiences from a disability studies perspective that seeks to problematize a heavy focus on individualized medical approaches to food allergies, especially where allergy testing and treatments are expensive and inaccessible for many people of color. It explores the multiple meanings of food allergies and eating in the United States.

Even though people we encounter online in U.S. food allergy communities and in publications like *Allergic Living* are mostly white, food allergy affects people of color more than white people. Black children are 7 percent more likely than white children to have food allergies. Asian and Pacific Islander/Native Hawaiian children are 24 percent and 26 percent more likely, respectively, to have food allergies than white children.[1] Yet representations of food allergy are continually whitewashed, as public awareness campaigns, illustrations in children's books, and ads for "allergen-free" foods feature white children. Racism in the food allergy community prioritizes the experiences, pain, struggles, and losses of white children and parents. Even though many adults also have food allergies, the representation of children continues to take the focus on interventions in school as a primary site for allergy activism. There are exceptions to these representations, yet the overwhelming imagination of a food-allergic child is a young white child, often with blonde hair. The food allergy advocacy and research community often focuses on and highlights the experiences of white individuals for legislative and funding gain, promoting food allergies as a condition that affects white children.[2]

Forwarding only whiteness in discussions of food allergies fails to challenge structural inequalities in which Black, Latinx, Indigenous, Asian, and other children and adults of color continue to experience limited access to testing, prescription drugs, and safe food options, and exclusion from food allergy communities. As an example, one study showed that Black and Hispanic children in the United States had a higher rate of anaphylaxis compared with their white counterparts. The Food Equality Initiative, one of only a handful of food assistance programs that provide allergen-free food, launched the 7 Percent Fund in 2020 to address "racial and economic inequalities within the food allergy community." On average, the total estimated costs associated with food allergy in the United States, including medical expenses, food costs, and lost renumeration because of unpaid care expenses, are $24.8 billion annually (which corresponds to $4,184 per child).[3] Structural racism and economic disparities often mean that for those without racial and economic privilege, the cost of food allergies—on top of other expenses—proves difficult to shoulder. People who cannot fill autoinjector prescriptions regularly hope that expired ones, or over-the-counter antihistamine pills, or even just avoidance of allergens, will work. Consistent allergy testing, desensitization and allergy shots, and updates of allergy plans also might be unavailable to those without affordable medical care, or who live in more rural spaces. For many families, especially those who are low income, the expensive and often smaller package of allergen-free cookies or cereal, for example, might not be available and will not get purchased. With each barrier or lack of opportunity comes increased risk for allergic reaction and potentially death.

The work of the Food Equality Initiative, and other groups like it across the country, is vital to ensure that those without consistent access to allergen-free food can receive supplies and foods that are safe, nutritious, and enjoyable. In June of 2020, Emily Brown, founder and then CEO of Food Equality Initiative, posted an "Open Letter to the Food Allergy Community" addressing the systemic racism and structural barriers she and other people of color experience in accessing resources and having their perspectives and expertise appreciated and understood. Brown's open letter joins similar statements from Black women before her, like Audre Lorde's open letter challenging Mary Daly's racist and generalizing treatment of Black women and her overall ignorance about the varied women-of-color goddesses in Daly's book *Gyn/Ecology*: "So the question arises in my mind, Mary, do you ever really read the work of Black women? Did you ever read my words, or did you merely finger through them for quotations which you thought might valuably support an already conceived idea concerning some old and distorted connection between us? This is not a rhetorical question." Lorde articulates the intersectional differences that Daly's work does not address, including a higher fatality rate for nonwhite women due to breast cancer, and high rates of unnecessary hysterectomies and sterilizations, and "three times as many chances for being raped, murdered, or assaulted" compared with white women. She also addresses the necessity of attending to differences among race, class, sexuality, and geography, and the dangers of a single-identity focus that obfuscates structural oppression and the manifestations of white supremacy. Lorde ends her letter to Daly with the following:

> I had decided never again to speak to white women about racism. I felt it was wasted energy because of destructive guilt and defensiveness, and because whatever I had to say might better be said by white women to one another at far less emotional cost to the speaker, and probably with a better hearing. But I would like not to destroy you in my consciousness, not to have to. So as a sister Hag, I ask you to speak to my perceptions. Whether or not you do, Mary, again I thank you for what I have learned from you. This letter is in repayment.[4]

Lorde's challenge is an important reminder that epistemological knowledge and insights generated from BIPOC (Black, Indigenous, People of Color) individuals should not be co-opted by white scholars and activists; instead, centering the need to dismantle interlocking systems of oppression requires attention to the ways in which activism might uphold white supremacy. Professional allergy researchers and allergy activists, myself included, must interrogate how focusing on single-experience politics and research without attending to the multiplicity of experience and locations of oppression can further jeopardize the lives of allergic and disabled people of color.

In her open letter, Emily Brown writes, "I found it very difficult to find the words and respond to questions from white colleagues and friends. How am I? I am not okay. Hearing yet another black voice ignored ending in George Floyd's death has triggered a familiar feeling, *the deep sorrow of grief.*" Brown documents her lifetime experience with racism—from being unable to order pizza with her sister and father as a child to being told that her own child's needs as a Black child with food allergies were "not a priority" by a "national food allergy patient advocacy group." She concludes, "My voice and family were ignored." Brown documents how this experience of being ignored, of trying to access allergen-safe foods but not finding assistance, led her to found the Food Equality Initiative to help end racial disparities in the food allergy community. All too often food allergy is framed as a condition that affects white and light-skinned individuals, especially those from middle- and upper-class backgrounds who experience barriers at exclusive sleepaway camps, in international travel, or during study-abroad opportunities. The day-to-day barriers to securing resources are not as regularly reported on, Brown writes:

> For far too long, white-led patient advocacy organizations have been hyper-focused on alleviating the challenges of the privileged and have failed to listen to the needs and priorities of patients who bear the overwhelming burden of the disease.
>
> These failures reinforce health disparities that manifest in limited access to care and treatments, allergen-free foods, and emergency epinephrine.
>
> Black children with food allergies are more likely to die from anaphylaxis than white children with food allergies. These Black Lives Matter!
>
> *Our voices, our families, and our health can no longer be ignored. We must take action.*[5]

Firmly asserting that the lives of Black individuals who have experiences of food allergy matter, Brown, like Lorde, is calling out the racism and violence that still exist in advocacy, media, and support organizations and groups.

The 7 Percent Fund, discussed above, was launched shortly after Brown released her letter. The Food Equality Initiative held a webinar, "For the Health: A Conversation on Race and Food Allergy," in which leading Black voices in food allergy advocacy came together to share their expertise and visions for elevating BIPOC leadership in food allergy communities, and for creating dialogues that invite white allies to monetarily support their efforts at creating lasting change and dismantling barriers to access and support.[6] Dina and Thomas Silvera shared their experiences of advocating to create Elijah's Law, named after their son Elijah Alavi-Silvera, who passed away due to anaphylaxis after being fed a grilled cheese sandwich in his New York City preschool, despite Elijah's documented allergies.[7] Elijah's Law requires daycare programs to "implement guidelines to prevent, recognize and respond to anaphylactic reactions." The panelists discussed the need to elevate Black voices, expertise, and experiences within organizations, research efforts, and various support groups. Brown made an impassioned plea that any effort connected to food allergies, from university research to initiatives undertaken at private medical practices, food production companies, and nonprofits, must begin to center antiracism in order to alter what are called the social determinants of health. These include economic and social circumstances that affect access to resources, and health care services and group differences in overall levels of health.[8]

The racism that Brown challenges in food allergy advocacy communities has a less-known history that interlocks with eugenics. As an example,

Dr. Charles Richet (1850–1935) is credited for his work on anaphylaxis. His research helped expand understanding of the role of proteins in causing allergic reactions in mammals. He was awarded the Nobel Prize in Physiology or Medicine in 1913. Richet was also an advocate of eugenics, arguing for the sterilization of individuals with intellectual disabilities and the racial superiority of white individuals. His Nobel acceptance speech argued that the "preservation of the race" is needed by allowing those with anaphylaxis to perish. In the biography of Richet posted to the Nobel Prize website, his eugenic racist beliefs are not mentioned.[9]

I write my own open letter to Richet grappling with the racist, eugenicist history of the celebrated physician. Food allergy is not a condition without a history. Part of the history of food allergy is the history of white supremacy, eugenics, and ableism. Although Richet cannot receive and reply to this letter, it is my attempt to continue the work of challenging the racist and eugenic history of the knowledge and treatment of anaphylaxis and food allergies, and their ongoing presence and impacts in these disciplines.

Dear Dr. Charles Richet,

I am in the middle of my fourth decade of life. As far back as I can remember, I have always been allergic to various tree nuts. One of my earliest memories is having a scratchy throat and difficulty breathing after eating part of a Brazil nut. Throughout my childhood and early adulthood, I had multiple accidental encounters with various nuts that led me to the emergency room. You described this as "heightened sensitivity" in your 1913 lecture after receiving the Nobel Prize, which was awarded for your research on anaphylaxis. But this is not a thank you letter. I feel compelled to write to you and challenge the racist, eugenic rhetoric you espoused to justify the significance of your research.

I have had anaphylactic reactions multiple times. Chances are I'll have more. I hope I don't die because of this type of reaction, but I suppose I might. I am "more fragile and susceptible," as you stated about allergic individuals. I'm one tiny piece of pine nut away from having a fatal reaction, as I live in a society that believes that the food allergic, or immunocompromised, or even the sick, are naturally deviant or deficient.

Dr. Richet, as I was reading your lecture, I was shocked by what you wrote: "There is something more important than the salvation of the person and that is integral preservation of the race." Because you were the head of the French Eugenics Society, your comments illustrate how white supremacy and ableism render disabled people of color expendable. You continued, quickly generalizing the (white) race as representing the species: "In other words, to formulate the hypothesis in somewhat abstract terms but clear ones all the same: *the life of the individual is less important than the stability of the species.* Anaphylaxis, perhaps a sorry matter for the individual, is necessary to the species, often to the detriment of the individual. The individual may perish, it does not matter. The species must at any time keep its organic integrity intact. Anaphylaxis defends the species against the peril of adulteration." But Dr. Richet, really, would the death of the allergic "defend" the human species? Your argumentation is oppressive and downright deadly, both then and now. The age of racist and ableist science is not some relic of our collective past. White supremacy and ableism are alive and well.

After discussing the necessity for individual "humoral personalities" to preserve genetic diversity, you stated, "It does indeed seem absurd that an organic disposition should make beings more fragile, more susceptible to poisons, for in most cases everything in living beings seems disposed to assure them a greater power of resistance." Why do you assume fragility is to be avoided? Can't we imagine that the multiplicity of living organisms means that some beings need extra protection? Or that what is assumed to be fragility might not always be? Quite frankly, it is absurd how you assume to know the truth of all bodies even though there are many ways of being and living. Bodies function and interact with others in new, inventive, and unimaginable ways.

Allergies and allergic reactions are but mere moments away. Many of us live with the reality of this precarity. One of the first things I do at grocery stores or restaurants is to look at labels, or to inquire about the presence of nuts, but there are always moments of miscommunication or mistakes. I often eat in places where my specific allergens are present. I take risks all the time. If I were to die, it might be tragic, but not some sign of evolution protecting the racial purity or the species.

I don't know if a cure for allergies will manifest in my lifetime, and I am not passively waiting for it. I live in a country that considers access to health care a privilege and not a right. If and when cures emerge, we have to make sure that they become widely available and free to all. White supremacist capitalism is a killing force. Without struggles to change these circumstances, the cures will likely first go to those white folks who can afford them. Not all allergic people are rich. Allergies are not the only precarity of our living conditions. There are economic and racial disparities, especially in access to safe food and water and also in access to treatment, including emergency room visits. As a white man from a family of modest means, I have survived potentially fatal reactions because of this privileged access to emergency care. Due to systemic injustice on multiple levels, many do not survive their allergic reactions and will not benefit from a cure unless this injustice is eliminated. Even if there were a cure, the need for accessible and just eating choices will continue to expand. The need for toxin-free work and living environments will continue.

We cannot separate food allergies from other human conditions and systems that imperil impoverished brown, Black, and Indigenous people, and people of color with and without disabilities. The perils of injustice are a killing force. We fight to ensure that everyone regardless of social location or financial resources can access medical care and safe food to mitigate this precarity. Thanks to the advocacy and bravery of leaders of color in allergy communities, questions of access and treatment are being raised and challenges to legacies of structural inequality are being made. Following the example of disability justice leaders, I demand that our classrooms, bedrooms, and public spaces become nurturing environments, and that we center the experiences and desires of disabled people of color, including those with allergies. Many are working hard to undo the white supremacy and racist medicine that you contributed to and were rewarded for. People are working hard to undo the systems of domination in our classrooms, exam rooms, labs, pantries, commercial kitchens, grocery stores, and streets. We do this work to undo what you started.

In defiance,
Mike Gill

ALLERGIC INTIMACIES

Introduction
Why Food Allergies?

In this book, I explore the multiple meanings of food allergies in the United States, including the ways in which structural inequalities prevent allergic people of color from accessing medical care, allergen-free food, diagnosis, and allergen-free spaces, and how allergic individuals make choices balancing risk with pleasure. I argue that food allergies are disabilities, and that managing food allergies, especially with the assumption that it requires individualized accommodations and privatized approaches, is disabling. Food allergies are on the rise, and an estimated thirty-two million Americans, including one in thirteen children, have food allergies. Diagnoses of food allergies in children have increased by 50 percent since 1997. Peanut allergies in particular tripled from 1997 to 2008. An often-cited statistic is that every three minutes, a food allergy reaction requires a visit to the emergency room.[1] There is great disparity in access to testing and treatment, with African American and Latinx children having higher risk of adverse outcomes than white children, including more rates of anaphylaxis.[2] There are very few studies that try to determine how food allergy varies across populations, including different populations of race and gender. One meta-analysis determined that self-reporting has increased, especially among Black children.[3] A study based on records at Mt. Sinai Hospital reports that more Black children were treated for food allergy during the time frame reviewed.[4] The article addresses a large sample (9,184 children), but only 3.4 percent (313) had a documented food allergy, which is significantly lower than the estimated rate of 7.6 percent of children with food allergies.

There remain many unknowns about how food allergy varies across populations. What is known is that food allergy testing and treatment remain expensive, and for children of color in the United States there remains a significant gap between access to testing and consistent treatment options. A 2013 article estimates that the cost of children's food allergies in the United States is $24.8 billion annually ($4,184 per child).[5] The costs include those related to medical treatments, prescription drugs, specialty foods, and caregiving.

Most research discusses food allergies in children. However, a recent study estimates that one in ten adults in the United States has a food allergy, although one in five adults believes they do. In addition, half of all adults developed an allergy during adulthood. This recent research on adults challenges assumptions that food-allergic individuals grow out of their allergies. For example, the increased prevalence of shellfish allergies in adults requires greater inquiry. Overall, there seems to be a significant number of food allergies in the United States. Rates of food allergies also seem to be increasing globally, with an estimate of 2.18 percent of the global population having a food allergy. Yet prevalence varies greatly by allergen; for example, 2.5 percent of all children in the United Kingdom are allergic to eggs, while only 0.07 percent of children in Greece are.[6] Despite these studies of prevalence, there remains much to be researched regarding food allergy. The meanings of food allergy are many, layered, and actively shaped by discourses of risk, vulnerability, and safety. Much like the varied and fluid meanings of other chronic conditions and disabilities, food allergies do not remain static but are constructed through political, cultural, and social processes, as well as through scientific knowledge.

A food-induced allergic reaction is the result of the immune system attacking the proteins found in what is often called an "offending food." The first time the body encounters the allergen, antibodies, in particular immunoglobulin E (IgE), are released and attach themselves to the body's mast and basophil immune cells. While these cells are found throughout the body, they are concentrated in the gastrointestinal (GI) tract, nose, skin, throat, lungs, and blood cells. When the allergen is next consumed, IgE binds with the allergen, producing histamine. This moment is when the various markers of allergy are produced, including tissue swelling, trouble breathing, GI issues, or, in the most severe cases, anaphylaxis, a potentially fatal allergic reaction. This description of an allergic reaction gives rise to discussions of immune responses as resembling warfare, with the "self" (the body) being defended from the "nonself" (allergen).

Emily Martin explores the limitations of considering the immune system in these militaristic terms. Among the many experts Martin interviews, two immunologists offer responses that provide salient insights about the relationship between the body, toxins/allergens/germs, and the immune system. Allan Chase, in discussing alternatives to military analogies, argues, "I could think of saying that your body's immune system functions as an interface between the human body and the environment. . . . I mean, that's a way of saying that you automatically are going to interact with your environment, and there are certain things that are hostile to the human body, and you can understand how the metaphor was generated, the 'defense' and everything. But actually, if you think about it, it gets a little carried away." Aaron Hunter draws a contrast with warfare: "[Microbes] are not just soldiers attacking us in the sense of attacking the U.S. They are just living their lives because they happen to live their lives in us. Plenty of organisms live their lives happily with us. Warfare is a very nice way to explain it on a very superficial level, but a normal part of existence as microorganisms is balance." In discussing the multiple meanings of immunity, Mel Y. Chen remarks how immune systems are "constituted by the intertwinings of scientific, public, and political cultures together."[7]

Predicting what will prompt a future reaction or illness requires calculations of things that might not always be calculable. In discussing environmental illness, Stacy Alaimo offers insight into how chemicals and other substances might produce illness and death, yet for some the need to balance what is dangerous and what is essential might appear to complicate a task: "The treatment for environmental illness thrusts the patient into the onto-epistemological terrain of contemporary risk society, where the ordinary citizen must assess a multitude of potential dangers—confronting vertiginous sources of information, colliding with objects and substances that seem to morph from benign to malignant."[8]

Further complicating these calculations, Mel Y. Chen adds, "Environmental toxicity and environmental degradation are figured as slow and dreadful threats to flesh, mind, home, and state." These threats are framed as jeopardizing a sense of well-being and even bodily autonomy. Yet, as Chen remarks, these "toxins" are not applied universally. Viruses, toxins, and other threats are constructed as "foreign" to white normative subjectivity. The violent increase in anti-Asian sentiment demonstrates the fatal consequences that Chen describes. Chen cautions, "Toxins participate vividly in the racial mattering of locations, human and nonhuman bodies, living and inert entities, and events such as disease threats."[9] Which bodies are assumed to be "at risk" is never a neutral claim, especially in a society where access to health care is determined by resources and by the willingness of medical professionals to believe what you say you know about your body. In discussing allergies, including theories of origin, the cultural and political dimensions of the allergen are often not forwarded. As I discuss in Chapter 1, for example, the peanut becomes linked rhetorically to "Americanness," yet its history as a crop of subsistence for enslaved persons is not acknowledged. Instead, peanut bans and discussions of peanut allergies continue to utilize the experiences and pain of the white child who has food allergies, despite individuals from all racial and ethnic categories having peanut allergies. As Emily Brown reminds us in her open letter (discussed in the Preface), all too often the representation and interventions suggested are assumed to benefit only white children, reinforcing white supremacy.

Questions of origin emerge when we consider why more individuals are being diagnosed with food allergies. When I introduce food allergy as my research topic, people often remark to me that food allergy is a contemporary phenomenon; they assume that previous generations did not have widespread food allergies. Embedded in these remarks are additional assumptions that the immune systems of children are too sensitive, and that highly processed foods are the reason for food allergies. In addition, some of these theories attempt to understand how some foods, like peanuts, appear to affect some folks in some locations but not others. One of these theories centers on the presence or absence of parasitic worms. Moises Velasquez-Manoff explores whether parasites might prevent allergic and autoimmune diseases. He explains that he infected himself with parasitic worms to see if they would help cure his various allergies (seasonal and food) and autoimmune diseases (including alopecia). He did get some relief from his seasonal allergies for a while, and small hairs started to grow on his head, but overall he wasn't "cured." However, his eczema disappeared, prompting him to guess that the period during which he had intestinal worms (about a year) did something for his immune system. Medical doctor James Logan, who has an allergy that prevents him from eating gluten, also purposely infected himself with hookworms as part of the U.K.-based television show *Embarrassing Bodies*. Despite the severe stomach pain associated with the self-infection, Logan could eat pizza and breadsticks: "Maybe the worms are having a good effect on my body. I am able to do things like eat bread, which is great."[10] Ultimately both Logan and Velasquez-Manoff ended their experiments, yet many individuals consider an occasional parasitic worm infection essential in helping to keep the immune system from becoming too sensitive.

Helminth (parasitic worm) exposure—or lack thereof—is only one of multiple hypotheses regarding why it seems that rates of allergic reaction have skyrocketed. The hygiene hypothesis is another popular explanation for why it seems some children have allergies and others do not. It states that early exposure to a multitude of microorganisms protects the child from developing allergies. According to Matthew Smith, the hygiene hypothesis suggests "that since children live in pristine, antiseptic environments and thus are not exposed to many pathogens, their immune systems are ill prepared to determine harmful proteins from harmful or nutritious ones." Mark Jackson adds that proponents of this hypothesis argue that lower levels of infection result in "immature immunological reactions." Having siblings, living on a farm, playing in the dirt, and having pets are all assumed to boost the immune systems of children. Yet there is not universal agreement that exposure to microorganisms helps prevent food allergy. Perhaps most authoritatively, Kari Nadeau and Sloane Barnett write, "The hygiene hypothesis isn't the complete solution to the mystery of food allergy. It's crucial to note that the studies behind the theory don't focus on food allergy. And although the nitty-gritty workings of the immune system may be the same for hay fever, eczema, and food allergy, the triggers may not be the same."[11] The research is inconclusive that being exposed to more "messy" or "dirty" environments protects an individual from developing food allergies. Quite simply, the immune system is incredibly complex, and simplistic approaches cannot account for the unpredictability of bodies in communication with environments.

There are other hypotheses why children develop food allergies, especially allergies to peanuts. Coming from an observation that children in some countries do not have high rates of peanut allergies, while others do, various groups of researchers have studied whether early and frequent exposure to peanuts lowers the overall number of allergies. The LEAP (Learning Early About Peanut Allergy) Study was a randomized trial that significantly reduced the prevalence of peanut allergy by giving children ground up peanut snacks (sometimes known as Bamba). At sixty months of age, around 13.7 percent of the children that avoided peanuts had an allergy to them, while in the consumption group only 1.9 percent had peanut allergy. People feeding newborns—or carrying fetuses—are told not to avoid peanuts and other allergens; however, other studies discuss the importance of consistently feeding newborns only breast milk to avoid triggering food allergies.[12] It appears that introducing peanuts early can help reduce the risk of food allergy. This is a reversal of early recommendations to avoid introducing allergens early, including before birth. Chances are that with additional studies more recommendations will emerge. Yet at this point, there still remains uncertainty regarding why some children develop food allergies and others do not, even within the same family.

Like faulty—but still widely circulated—conjectures regarding links between vaccines and autism, some parents of children with food allergies, especially to peanuts, circulate hypotheses bordering on conspiracy, that link vaccines to allergies. Heather Fraser's The Peanut Allergy Epidemic: What's Causing It and How to Stop It is perhaps the most widely read and cited text making this link. Fraser (and others) argue that peanut oil adjuvants (substances used in vaccines to enhance an immune response) were approved by the FDA for use in vaccines. As proof of the link Fraser miscites a New York Times article that reported on the clinical testing of a vaccine using Adjuvant 65 (which contained peanut oil), but Adjuvant 65 was never approved for widespread usage, and there are no records of peanut oil being used in vaccines.[13]

Questions about the origin of food allergies will evolve. As will the collective understanding regarding frequency of allergies ("Why are children increasingly being diagnosed with sesame allergies?" "How come adults are developing shellfish allergies?"). When I was first diagnosed with severe food allergies around four decades ago, the knowledge about food allergies was limited. My parents received the advice to have me avoid all allergens. Based on one reaction where I threw up after eating peanut butter, I was told I was allergic to peanuts. It was not until over thirty years later, when I had decent health insurance with a low copay, enabling food allergy testing, that I found out I was not actually allergic to peanuts. (I even went through an in-office food challenge where I was served peanut butter in increasing doses to make sure I did not have a reaction. To further complicate this narrative, a more recent blood test indicated peanut as an allergen.) Yet after avoiding for so long a food I was told I could not eat, to this day I have not sought out peanuts or peanut products. I have lived as an individual who avoids peanuts out of fear of an allergic reaction. To this day the smell of roasted peanuts makes my throat itch, even if that itch is connected to years of anxiety and is not explained by an immune response. As Nadeau and Barnett argue, "Genetics, environment, upbringing, eating habits, and so much more contribute to the full picture of each individual food allergy. Food allergy prevention and treatment isn't a one-size-fits-all practice."[14]

Our immune systems are constantly processing and communicating with a wide variety of substances. Many of these are benign, posing no immediate threat. Yet, as Chen and Alaimo show, these moments of engagement between substances and the immune system are cumulative and potentially require the individual to consider how their bodies might react in the future. Therefore, safeguarding against these threats by identifying and avoiding substances cannot guarantee safety. Dayna Glabau cautions against relying solely on technological fixes to address food allergy, such as devices that can identify the presence of allergens in prepared food because of the messiness and unpredictability of bodies.[15]

Along with discussions of origin, another main focus of food allergy research has been about advancing cures. Recently the FDA approved a peanut desensitization drug, Palforzia, which provides children from age four to seventeen the opportunity to incrementally consume peanut protein made from defatted peanut flour. This incremental exposure starts at 0.5 milligrams (mg) of peanut. Successful treatment occurs over a period of six months, when the patient is consuming a daily dose of 300 mg of the drug, which is the equivalent of one peanut.[16] Palforzia is not about "curing" peanut allergy, but rather preventing anaphylaxis due to accidental exposure. Yet children who take the drug are risking anaphylaxis, so this type of treatment is risky in the present but potentially protective in the future.[17] The list price of the drug is $890 a month. It is unknown currently if the drug will be widely covered by all types of prescription drug insurance benefits. The manufacturer has created a patient support savings program that can cover copays up to $5,800 a year for eligible patients.[18] The price tag means that many peanut-allergic children will not be able to access this medication. Like injectable epinephrine, allergy testing, and processed foods free from allergens, the financial burden for food allergic individuals continues—not to help them be cured from allergies but rather to help prevent severe reactions that can lead to death. These technological advances and prescription drugs primarily benefit children from upper-middle-class, well-resourced families, which tend to be white families. Democratizing the resources and technologies of allergy testing and management can continue to shift the ways in which structural racism and economic inequality make only some children "savable."[19]

Critical scholarship exploring historical, political, and cultural dimensions of food allergy are being published. Scholars such as Danya Glabau and Matthew Smith are exploring historical and science and technological approaches to food allergy. I rely on their work here and in the chapters that follow to contextualize my work within broader historical and anthropological conversations about patients and access. Likewise, leading food allergy specialists Richi Gupta and Kari Nadeau have both cowritten recent texts summarizing clinical knowledge and food allergy management. These sources are invaluable, as are the clinical studies that these and other researchers have completed, when considering the complicated embodied experiences of those with food allergies. My own work expands the critical and clinical scholarship on food allergy by extending a disability studies analysis. The field of disability studies has not engaged with food allergy. My work begins to correct this imbalance by considering how individualized approaches to food allergy management remain insufficient insomuch as the medical and political forces of racism and ableism result in heightened food insecurity and insufficient access to medical treatments for people of color with food allergies.

In what follows, I discuss four scenarios of how food-allergic individuals and advocates seek to take control of their food allergies while managing costly treatments, inaccessible spaces, and a lack of legal recourse. In addition, these examples illuminate how single-issue approaches—for example, arguing only for generic epinephrine—are not sufficient to address the needs and desires of food-allergic people of color. I argue that racism and ableism create a unique precarity for disabled people of color that food-allergic communities are only beginning to address. Moving beyond individualized approaches to more robust coalitional efforts grounded in disability and racial justice can begin to shift these patterns of exclusion.

Scenario One: DIY Epinephrine Injectors

Epinephrine helps reverse the symptoms of anaphylaxis, a severe allergic reaction. The chemical, when injected, opens airways in the lungs and narrows blood vessels, allowing the person experiencing the allergic reaction an opportunity to travel to an emergency room for follow-up treatment. Those with severe allergies at risk of or with histories of anaphylaxis are encouraged to carry epinephrine as the main mode of treatment in the case of accidental ingestion of an allergen. As I discuss below, this medical-based solution is limited in that epinephrine is expensive and often not carried by the allergic individual.

Epinephrine is usually made available by prescription as an autoinjector, in which the medicine is delivered via a spring-loaded syringe through an intramuscular injection. The EpiPen, the oldest brand of injectors, was developed by Survival Technology in Bethesda, Maryland, in the 1970s. It was approved by the FDA to be marketed for treating anaphylaxis in 1987. As an allergic kid, I was first prescribed an EpiPen around the time it was approved by the FDA. For over ten years the EpiPen was available as a single-pack injector. In 2001, a double-pack injector was introduced. Mylan Pharmaceuticals acquired the rights for the EpiPen in 2007, and starting in 2009 the price steadily increased. In 2009, a twin pack cost $103 dollars, and by 2016 it cost $608, a 500 percent price increase. In the summer of 2016 outrage over the increased cost erupted as consumers and U.S. government officials began to demand oversight and more affordable generic versions of the drug. It was estimated that the cost to manufacture the twin pack is roughly ten dollars. Glabau argues that the increased price of the EpiPen is a "promissory orientation" and "hoped-for financial value" that these types of pharmaceuticals can generate for investors.[20]

The autoinjector is valid for a year, meaning that allergic individuals must annually refill their prescriptions. Also, because of various rules and regulations, school-age children often must have multiple valid prescriptions so there can be an injector at school, at after-school programs, and at home. Families might pay thousands of dollars annually for these refills. As of the summer of 2022, there were ongoing legal actions against Mylan. A class action lawsuit was settled in 2022.

Acting against the pharmaceutical industry's profiteering practices, consumers, medical practitioners, and activists have tried to circumvent medical insurance, pharmacy benefit managers, copays, and limited availability to democratize injectable epinephrine. These efforts, a type of creativity within revolt, are aligned with other efforts globally to make generic versions of pharmaceutical drugs available for those that cannot afford them.[21] Dr. Marcus Romanello, chief medical officer and emergency room physician at Ft. Hamilton Hospital, in Hamilton, Ohio, advocated for creating a ten-dollar epinephrine kit.[22] The kit involves an empty Altoids tin, a syringe, and a vial of epinephrine. In an interview, Romanello discussed his own family's experience with allergies—his older son has had to use an EpiPen for his tree nut allergy—as well as patients who "are literally having to choose between carrying a life-saving device and putting food on the table." Romanello says that although the patients have to be trained to use the syringe and vial, this solution is a more affordable and potentially accessible version for some allergic individuals. If individuals do inject "a little too much" of the epinephrine during anaphylaxis, it would not cause a problem.[23] One of the most common concerns about this approach is that individuals might not be able to correctly inject the medicine. Yet many individuals self-inject prescription drugs, including insulin and other hormones. Glabau argues, "Key moments in the life of a person with food allergies revolve around epinephrine: preparing for allergic reactions by learning to use the device, reorienting family and social life around food allergy preparedness, and going online to find support from others who have made it through apparently life-threatening reactions." In moments of severe reaction, I have been calm enough to manage injecting myself using an autoinjector. If people can learn how to use the autoinjector, they can be trained to manage a vial and syringe. Part of the training for this alternative injector can include making practice injections into oranges or other types of fruit or vegetables. For the food allergic, managing epinephrine is considered an "indicator of dutiful self-care."[24]

The biohacking anarchist collective known as Four Thieves Vinegar Collective released open-source plans for individuals to create an "EpiPencil." The collective writes, "WHEREAS The pharmaceutical industry continues to put profits above human life, and WHEREAS Autoinjectors and epinephrine are technology which belongs to the world, and WHEREAS EpiPens save lives every day, but only for those who can afford them, and SINCE The Four Thieves Vinegar Collective is dedicated to providing access to everyone WE HAVE developed the EpiPencil, an epinephrine autoinjector which can be built entirely using off-the-shelf parts, for just over $30 US." They directly challenge models of capitalism that link privatization of technological development and market monopolization. More recently Four Thieves has released an apothecary microlab, a device that allows users to create multiple medications, including ones to treat malaria and to counteract opioid overdose. The founder of Four Thieves, Michael Laufer, volunteered in El Salvador during graduate school. A nurse he worked with told him that the clinic had run out of antibiotics and birth control medication. Laufer thought the clinic should be able to make its own medicine to solve the problems of access and cost.[25]

The Four Thieves Collective takes its name from a group of thieves and grave robbers in medieval Europe who protected themselves from the plague by placing in their masks a mixture of vinegar and herbs that were thought to have have antimicrobial properties. Recipes for so-called four thieves vinegar appear all over the internet. Common and widely available herbs like angelica and rosemary are infused in vinegar to create culinary ingredients, products for skin care, or household cleaning solutions.[26] On its website, the collective offers instructions via text and video on how to source materials and assemble the EpiPencil. The original video was posted to YouTube but was later removed for supposedly violating "community guidelines"; however, the collective has posted links to the archived videos, including the original and a follow-up version highlighting answers to frequently asked questions. The instructions for the EpiPencil are quite straightforward, illustrating how user friendly (and nontechnical) the device can be. Romanello also stresses user-friendliness with his version of the reusable mint-tin vial and syringe.

Here are instructions from the Four Thieves Vinegar Collective for the EpiPencil:

0) Print the label, and affix it to the autoinjector.
1) Remove the 22 gauge luer-lock needle from its associated syringe, if it is affixed to one.
2) Press-fit the needle onto the 1 milliliter luer-slip syringe.
3) Depress the plunger on the autoinjector using the barrel, until it clicks.
4) Set the depth adjuster between 7 and 15 millimeters depending on your subcutaneous layer, and how heavy your clothing tends to be.
5) Carefully remove the cap from the needle which is now affixed to the syringe.
6) Draw .3 milliliters of epinephrine into the syringe.
7) Inspect carefully to make sure there are no air bubbles, and remove them if present.

8) Being careful not to touch the needle to the sides, gently insert the syringe and needle into the barrel of the autoinjector.

9) Screw the handle onto the autoinjector.

The autoinjector is now loaded and complete. Store in a safe, sterile container, away from the sun, but not in the refrigerator.

STAY HEALTHY,

—THE FOUR THIEVES VINEGAR COLLECTIVE

The collective's label for the EpiPencil is an obvious spoof of the EpiPen label, with some notable differences. For example, the label instructs the user "Don't panic!" and also states that this is "an open-source medical device." Resisting the need to use a trademark and any claim of proprietary property, efforts like the creation of the EpiPencil seek to allow allergic individuals to take greater control over their allergy management.[27]

Similarly, Dr. Cathleen London, a family medicine physician in Maine, created her own version of an epinephrine autoinjector using insulin pens, which under normal circumstances allow patients to self-inject a premeasured amount of insulin. The workings of the pens, which London sells to her patients for $50, are very similar to those of the EpiPencil. London charges her patients $2.50 to refill the pen after using it, or to replace expired epinephrine.[28]

In the follow-up to the Four Thieves FAQ video, Laufer explains that there are many other efforts underway to create alternatives to the EpiPen. One of these is AllergyStop, a keychain-size injector under development by an allergist who himself has food allergies, Douglas McMahon. In an interview with *Minnesota Medicine*, McMahon discusses how the device should not cost more than $50 because he wants "this in patients' hands. I don't need to be sitting on a yacht drinking piña coladas all day. If we make a profit, great. But getting this out to people is our main goal."[29]

An undergraduate student at Rice University, Justin Tang, proposed a wearable option, EpiWear. Tang and his teammates created a prototype for the device, hoping to market a version like a watch like that could be taken apart and assembled. Tang is allergic to peanuts and requires injectable epinephrine; however, he admits he forgets to carry his device. He also says the rigidity and bulkiness of an EpiPen makes it difficult to carry. The EpiWear prototype could be unfolded into a pen injector. Tang tried to find investors for the EpiWear but encountered difficulty navigating the complicated maze of patents and FDA approval.[30]

Teenagers often remark how larger devices are more difficult to carry. A recent study found that roughly 44 percent of food-allergic individuals who require injectable epinephrine carry such devices consistently. In addition, only one-third of children and teenagers carry the devices. Tang mentioned speaking to many allergic individuals who were very interested in a wearable option. Finding a solution that works for more users becomes a priority. The EpiWear and similar devices can meet a desperate need for individuals to have consistent, wearable access to epinephrine. The Auvi-Q injector is a credit-card-sized device that one study reports more people carry regularly than pen-type injectors.[31]

As long as those at risk of anaphylaxis are not consistently able to access the medication because of cost, availability, or easy of portability, then allergic individuals continue to navigate the world while remaining at risk of having an allergic reaction. Chapter 4 discusses how, each year, multiple food-allergic individuals die as a result of accidental ingestion of the allergen; more often than not these individuals are not carrying injectable epinephrine.

Efforts to create more autoinjectors, or to diversify delivery of epinephrine, attempt to place the tools of allergy management into the hands of consumers. In the various journalistic accounts that discuss these devices, there are cautionary notes that these interventions are risky. Of course, many folks manage vials and syringes to inject hormones and other prescription drugs. By asserting the risk attached to using these non-FDA approved devices, the medical voice of authority is able to label allergic individuals, physicians, and biohackers promoting the products as jeopardizing the health and safety of "the vulnerable." As Judith Butler asks, "The dependency on infrastructure for a livable life seems clear, but when infrastructure fails, and fails consistently, how do we understand that condition of life?" When this vulnerability is constructed as a private, apolitical condition (e.g., diabetes or food allergies) that is resolved through relationships between "patients," "doctors," and prescription drugs, with insurance companies, pharmacy benefit managers, and countless others privy to medical information, this supposed private relationship is actually quite intricate and a structure of interdependency upon others. Sherene Razack argues that labeling someone vulnerable is tautological; someone is vulnerable because they have always been vulnerable. Razack discusses how the conditions of vulnerability that are social and structural are attributed to the individual's weakness. Eunjung Kim adds, "Privatized vulnerability is the key in constructing power and difference, as the determination of subjects as vulnerable can make them vulnerable."[32] These supposedly "vulnerable" individuals who are dependent on epinephrine are seeking to challenge a system that requires compliance with increasing copays, limited access, and allergic calculations where the price of prescription drugs means other essentials like utilities and food are sacrificed.

The medicine needed to maintain life—be it epinephrine, insulin, or something else—often costs very little to produce and can be easily offered to more individuals. Indeed, the Open Insulin Project, like the Four Thieves Vinegar Collective, describes itself as "a team of Bay Area biology nerds who believe that insulin should be freely available to anyone who needs it." Similar to the EpiPen, the price for vials of insulin has risen dramatically. A vial of Humalog produced by Eli Lilly cost twenty-one dollars in 1996. The same vial in 2019 cost $324.[33] Comparable to allergic people using expired epinephrine or going without, one in four diabetics rations insulin, putting their lives in jeopardy. Senator Bernie Sanders has traveled with diabetics from the United States to Canada to purchase insulin to highlight how prescription drug profits in the United States prevent many people from accessing a life-sustaining medication. The price structure of both insulin and epinephrine injectors disproportionately affects economically disadvantaged communities, especially communities of color in areas of concentrated poverty with long histories of redlining, racial segregation, and limited access to reliable, affordable health care. Outside the United States, the price of a vial of insulin varies greatly, but more often than not diabetics in the United States spend more than diabetics in other countries to obtain their medication. EpiPens dramatically vary in cost as well; a twin pack costs sixty-nine dollars in the United Kingdom.[34]

I close this section by describing two posts that Bernie Sanders shared during his 2020 presidential campaign. The first is a two-part Instagram post from December 11, 2019, which comes with this caption: "This is what happened when people in the U.K. were quizzed about the cost of health care in America. They literally cannot believe what they are hearing. We cannot be a nation that simply leaves the poor, sick, and unlucky to die. We need Medicare for All." An image attached to the caption shows a white man in the U.K. guessing the cost for two EpiPens in the United States. He guesses eighty dollars, which is on par with the cost in the U.K. He learns that the actual cost is $600, and looks very surprised. Similarly, a white woman guesses the price for an inhaler. She guesses $100, only to be informed that the actual price is $250 to $350. She replies, "For an inhaler? Man, so if you're poor, you're dead." Another Instagram post from Sanders reads, "Insulin costs 10 times more in the U.S. than in Canada. For the same damn product made by the same damn company, Americans are charged 10 times more. We are going to end that thievery in this country."[35]

Certainly, both posts highlight the price disparity between countries and how individuals with chronic conditions spend money for medication that sustains life or prevents death. Furthermore, these medications are not expensive to make, yet the profits they generate mean that more and more diabetics, allergic individuals, and other disabled, ill, or sick individuals lack consistent and reliable access to these medications. Butler avers:

> We cannot talk about a body without knowing what supports that body and what its relation to that support—or lack of support—might be. In this way, the body is less an entity than a relation, and it cannot be fully dissociated from the infrastructural and environmental conditions of its living. Thus, the dependency of human and other creatures on infrastructural support exposes a specific vulnerability that we have when we are unsupported, when those infrastructural conditions characterizing our social, political, and economic lives start to decompose, or when we find ourselves radically unsupported under conditions of precarity or under explicit conditions of threat.[36]

To challenge these conditions of precarity, biohacking and democraticizing certain medicines remain necessary types of creative revolt to allow others to live. The allergic and diabetic individuals at the center of these efforts are using their disabled and impaired lives—and their dependencies on prescription drugs and insurance coverage—to shift the assumption that chronicity demands acquiescence. Using crowdfunding, off-the-shelf parts, hacking, and social media, these activists are demanding consistent access to drugs that belong to us all.

Scenario Two: Please Don't Eat Here; or, What Is an Allergic Person to Do?

Right under the cash register is the following sign: "We use many allergens including eggs, dairy, peanuts, and tree nuts in many of our baked goods. If you have a severe allergy, we recommend you don't eat anything and just enjoy tea or coffee." Another bakery offers the following: "Many of our products contain 8 of the most common allergens. Diners assume responsibility." Allergic individuals are familiar with the many types of allergen statements that indicate the potential for cross contamination. In an important article exploring the need for international frameworks on clear and consistent allergen-labeling practices, Katrina Allen and colleagues include a table of the most common phrases of advisory warnings. A quick scan of the chart shows the different ways to describe the process of manufacturing—from "may contain traces," to "made in a facility that also processes," to "produced on shared equipment which also processes," to "not suitable for . . . allergy sufferers."[37]

Sloane Miller, author of *Allergic Girl: Adventures in Living Well with Allergies*, prefers a certain type of statement: "That kind of 'no' is not 'We don't serve your kind here. . . . It is 'We do not have the facility yet to accommodate you and feel nervous for you, but we want you to stay. How can we make you comfortable?'"[38] For Miller, this communicates the admission of one's limitation but not a blanket refusal.

I would be more inclined to purchase an item that was made in a facility that also processes allergens than something that shared the same manufacturing equipment with an item containing nuts. I would also be more inclined to avoid consuming something that is labeled as not suitable for those with nut allergies, but I acknowledge frequenting and eating from a bakery that uses similar language in their statement. The allergic calculation at this moment in my journey means I am making eating decisions that are influenced by taste, desire, and pleasure (the bakery makes excellent bagels) as well as temporal distance from my last allergic reaction. Risk assessment is often personal, unscientific, and inconsistent. I've been steered toward certain dishes at restaurants when disclosing my allergies, and I've also avoided certain products and places because of the presence of allergens. I have only been refused service once because of my allergy. But if I was more explicit in describing my allergies and the risks involved, I am certain that I would be denied service, or only given the choice between coffee and tea.

Allergen warnings vary by location depending on what allergies are prevalent, what ingredients are commonly used, and how foods are classified. In Japan, only allergens that are predominantly found, like buckwheat and peanut, are required to be labeled, but others like dairy might not be labeled. Also, the presence of other foods like peaches, kiwi, and beef might also be labeled. In the European Union, pine nuts are considered seeds, whereas legislation in the United States (Food Allergen Labeling and Consumer Protection Act of 2004) considers pine nuts along with coconut and lychee, among others, to be tree nuts. None of these things are botanically classified as nuts, but instead as drupes, fruit, and seeds. To further complicate matters, there is limited understanding of why some people are allergic to only pine nuts but not tree nuts, and why others with tree nut allergies are also allergic to pine nuts. As labeling requirements change from country to country, allergens like sesame and mustard may be highlighted, or not even considered as producing reactions. By 2023, sesame must be listed as an allergen on products sold in the United States.[39]

The global movement of food products and globalization of cuisine allows for individuals to consume products that are baked, fried, or mixed miles away.

For example, I regularly buy and eat a brand of ramen noodles that are labeled as both vegan and halal certified. Sometimes these noodles are made in a factory in Korea. Other times the same noodles are made in a factory in the United States. Both factories also make products containing a variety of allergens and ingredients that are not vegan (milk, eggs) and not halal for some Muslims (crustacean shellfish).[40] I am intentionally bringing allergen-free eating into the conversation about other eating practices, including halal and vegan, to highlight how these statements and production practices affect a wide number of consumers. Accidentally eating animal products for a vegan can cause health problems, and eating items that are not halal can be a sin that requires repentance. Allergic individuals can expand our focus to discuss the need for all types of consumers to have robust and consistent labeling practices. If the noodles are made in a facility that processes products with other ingredients, are the noodles then vegan? The same question applies to halal foods. How does cross-contamination factor into certification, or consumer confidence? What choice might a vegan with an egg allergy make? Or someone who follows halal eating practices who is also allergic to dairy? Discussions of allergies might often focus on avoiding certain ingredients, but the many motivations for eating (or not eating) certain items means that the decisions we make might be much more complicated and inconsistent. The allergic calculation recognizes that decisions made are impacted by trusting the words and labels on the package (or provided by the restaurant establishment)—for example, once nut free always nut free. Eating safely and following certain eating practices require diligence and not making assumptions that what was once safe to consume will be safe the next time. Or not assuming that as a consumer you can trust the countless employees in factories, kitchens, and production lines to follow protocol and industry practices and regulations. With each bite, a small risk comes along.

Scenario Three: Not Cleared to Fly

Imagine getting ready to board an international flight home, and despite communicating to the airline multiple times that you have a severe allergy to apples, you are not allowed to board. Instead, you are taken to a small room, scolded by airline employees, and asked if your physician cleared you to fly. Or imagine that despite signing a waiver not holding the airline responsible, you are told that your peanut allergy prevents you from flying. You have to pay for a night in a hotel and book another flight while forfeiting the original flight. These are just a few of the many stories of individuals, including "Amanda" and Norine Khalil, who frankly detail how difficult or impossible it can be to travel with severe allergies. Some allergic individuals do not expect to be served an allergen-free meal, which are almost nonexistent, with the exception of gluten-free meals; rather, they want the airline to guarantee that their allergens (in particular peanuts) are not provided to others as snacks and that an announcement is made asking people to refrain from the allergen. Other passengers with allergies talk about having been told to wear a mask throughout the flight and not eat anything, or having to sit in the airplane bathroom to avoid exposure to allergens, while other passengers could freely eat and drink and did not have to wear a mask.[41] Masking takes on a different meaning during a pandemic, when all are required to wear masks on planes, yet eating and drinking still occurs, with the potential for allergens to become airborne.

Of course, individuals with food allergies are often told instead of flying to take a train, drive, or stay home. Immunocompromised persons are also told to avoid public transportation or flying; this is especially true during the pandemic. These impaired and sick bodies become hypervisible when they are refused boarding or told not to travel. As a result, many do choose to drive, or not to travel. But work, funerals, a family member's illness, vacations, and countless other events still go on, meaning that allergic folks and immunocompromised individuals might have to make a calculation where taking a risk with a potentially uncontrolled environment outweighs staying at home. This calculation is something the food allergic often make. Is it safe to eat here? Can I have this piece of cake? Should I bring my own food to the potluck, or skip it entirely? Sometimes the choice to skip (or not to partake) is an easy one to make—for example, if you have a peanut allergy, not going to a burger restaurant that fries everything in peanut oil and gives customers unlimited peanuts to shell and eat. But at other times the decision is more difficult, like determining which airline might be the safest and might have the most robust allergen policy (especially when food allergy policy enforcement often depends on individual staff, regardless of the airline's official protocols). Will fellow passengers be sympathetic, or will someone insist on eating their pistachios? I call this weighing of risks based on social and physical environments, temporality and proximity, and emotional and corporeal desires the "allergic calculation."[42] Those with food allergies are making decisions about what is safest for them, despite the inability to control their environments completely. Individuals can choose to avoid certain foods, or to not eat in certain situations, but having others around them might mean there is allergen nearby. Despite needing to act with determination to remain safe from reaction, there still remains uncertainty and risk.

In 1998 the U.S. Department of Transportation (DOT) recommended including three peanut-free rows on large U.S. airlines. Politicians, peanut farmers, and various commentators called into question the patriotism of those who advocate for peanut-free spaces. Some politicians, especially from Georgia, tried to link funding for the DOT to not banning peanuts on airplanes. As a result, the DOT has not made a ruling about banning peanuts on airplanes, although individual carriers are free to make that determination. The DOT issued an order in 2019 stating that prohibiting individuals with allergies from preboarding was a violation of the Air Carrier Access Act. This ruling, made against American Airlines, means it is easier to allow food-allergic individuals and accompanying family members to preboard flights to wipe down seats, trays, and other areas to rid surfaces of potential allergens. Most U.S.-based air carriers now allow those with allergies to preboard. In addition, the Americans with Disability Act Amendments Act of 2008 expanded the definition of disability, which is now widely held to encompass "severe" food allergies. However the law itself does not provide the standard for determining what is a "severe" food allergy. Likewise, these various laws often only consider disability as a single-identity issue that obfuscates the ways in which white privilege manifests itself. For example, an overwhelming majority of air passengers in the United States are white. The most recent data, from 2015, in a report posted to Airlines for America, a lobbying group of U.S. carriers, highlights that two-thirds of all travelers are white.[43] Further, considering the cost of air travel, the average passenger, including the passenger with food allergies, is white and middle to upper class. Food allergy activism continues to focus on safe airline travel as one of the central goals, yet those that have access to airplanes are often those with racial and class privileges that provide additional levels of safety, including the ability to be believed when disclosing an allergy to airline staff and the resources to purchase seating that offers more space. The work of food allergy activism can align with that of racial and economic justice to consider how expanding access to health insurance, injectable epinephrine, and subsidized allergen-free foods can improve the lives of a disabled people of color, including those with food allergies. Likewise, in focusing on the experiences of airline passengers with food allergies, food allergy activists can join with racial justice activists to call out and challenge racial profiling, including Islamophobia and anti-immigrant sentiment, which are exacerbated by heightened surveillance in airports.

Scenario Four: Nut-Free at the Gingham Altar

During season ten of *The Great British Bake Off* (GBBO), a hit Netflix series featuring amateur bakers competing in weekly baking challenges, a white contestant, Rosie Brandreth-Poynter, had a dedicated "nut runner, that made sure all the ingredients Brandreth-Poynter baked with were free from nuts." The runner also made sure all Brandreth-Poynter's equipment was cleaned and stored away from that of the other bakers to avoid cross-contamination. Viewers did not know about Brandreth-Poynter's runner or her severe allergy to nuts until she was eliminated in the semifinals and GBBO posted a thank you note from Brandreth-Poynter to Twitter. She wrote, "The crew was incredible—they managed my nut allergy so well and kept everything safe—including the awesome NUT RUNNER—how many people can put that on a CV?"[44] She won viewers over with her elaborate creations—including a chicken made out of 212 biscuits and a safari of bread that featured an elephant—and lots of witty back and forth with Noel Fielding, one of the show's cohosts. She is also remembered for dropping one of her blackberry custard tarts on the ground.

Anita Mannur writes in *Intimate Eating: Racialized Spaces and Radical Futures* that through GBBO, "the nation becomes an intimate space wherein baking together forms the basis of a shared vision of the future, one that runs contrary to the ideas of a separationist UK in a post-Brexit era." In her astute analysis, Mannur examines how "race plays an important part in defining what can be baked into quintessentially British fare," and traces how South Asian bakers, especially Nadiya Hussain, Tamal Ray, and Rahul Mandal, use South Asian spices to expand the limited palate (and imagination) of judges Paul Hollywood, Mary Berry, and Prue Leith. Mannur argues that "inside the tent," the possibility exists of a "newer and kinder nation—an intimate eating public in which the members of the nation bake together to imagine a better future for a nation riven by exclusion and division. It is at once predicated on a kind of false nostalgia for a happier, more gentle time and invested in the idea of a future culinary utopia." In the space under the tent with the gingham altar, where the imperialist history of the U.K. and the structural racism and efforts of exclusion are erased (or ignored), "stranger intimacy becomes possible and even celebrated because of an investment in the idea of a better good life."[45]

As a nut-allergic person, I am always interested to see representations of allergies on baking and cooking competition shows. As an interdisciplinary scholar that uses a variety of critical theories and texts in my writing and teaching, I'm also keenly interested in tracing how discourses of "multiculturalism" or "diversity" are used in discussions of representation, while real engagement with oppression and exclusion are ignored. GBBO is edited to create the atmosphere of genuine support and friendship among the contestants. The intimacy based on nationality that Mannur theorizes about seems to move beyond the tent. One of the more touching moments in season ten was when the remaining bakers wore ties the week after contestant Henry Bird was eliminated.[46] As Mannur argues, the bakers do what they do for pleasure, which might allow them to "build a better good life" and "a temporary salve from all the forms of inequality, despair and lack of hope"; she uses Lauren Berlant's term, "cruel optimism."[47]

Brandreth-Poynter going public with her allergy (discussing it on-screen) would have troubled the intimacy in the tent and changed how viewers responded to her, generating speculation that she was receiving an unfair advantage or being exposed to risk by the presence of nuts in the other bakes. Unlike the disabilities of contestants Marc Elliot, whose amputation was central to his baking journey, and Briony Williams, whose hand was often shown on-screen as she kneaded bread or mixed batters, viewers were not shown Brandreth-Poynter's disability experience. Both Elliot's and Williams's disabilities were captured on-screen. Viewers might have to confront their own ableism as these disabled contestants compete, or the inclusion of these contestants might create an inspirational narrative. Kim-Joy Hewlett only disclosed her anxiety and experiences with mutism in interviews conducted during the show. (Like Brandreth-Poynter's, Hewett's impairment might have been exacerbated in the tent.) There are probably other disabled contestants that have not disclosed their experiences. Overall, the editing of GBBO does not center disability experiences even if they show impairments on-screen. In an article for Anaphylaxis.org.uk, Brandreth-Poynter writes of her experience living with severe nut allergies. She tells of a time on a school trip to a chocolate factory when she had to wear a sign that read, "nut allergy. do not feed."[48] She was excluded from a trip to France with her classmates because the school said they could not accommodate for her. She was unable to obtain an affordable nut-free wedding cake, so her friends ended up baking one for her and her husband. She writes that her love of baking is directly affected by her and her younger sister's nut allergies—and a desire to eat nut-free baked goods. Her experience of exclusion creates an aspiration to facilitate allergen-free bakes and recipes for others.

Brandreth-Poynter writes,

> Applying to the Great British Bake Off felt like a slightly pointless
> activity; they were never going to take someone with an allergy over
> thousands of easier to manage applicants. I was completely upfront
> about my allergy, and about what I could and couldn't do from the
> start; I am ok with nuts in the same room (other than Brazil nuts) but
> I couldn't bake with them or handle them myself. The team were
> brilliant, phoning me several times to check exactly what I could do,
> and then, I got the best call ever—to say I'd made it into the tent![49]

Of note here is how she directly communicated exactly what the allergy entails. Common advice given to allergic individuals is to be up-front in communicating allergies to others, especially when food is being served or bought. Despite her communicating her needs, however, her allergy was erased from the final show. Under the large baking tent, an opportunity was wasted to highlight how planning and protocol are needed to ensure safety, ultimately resulting in a missed chance to emphasize that intentional planning and resources are often needed to fully include those with allergies in these types of spaces.

In this book, I explore how allergic individuals and their requirement for food (and possibly spaces) free of allergens can be taken up by all, potentially destabilizing discrete boundaries between individuals, immune systems, and desires. If I refuse to eat products with dairy in the presence of a person with a dairy allergy, and if I claim their need for dairy-free products as also necessary for me, then it matters very little who has the "real" allergy. What happens if, through the act of solidarity, we communicate the need for spaces and food that are not specialized or medicalized, but rather widely available? I understand that this shifts the individualized approach Western countries adopt regarding disability access. As Danya Glabau maintains, "Should we be seeking quick fixes for ailments of individual bodies? Or should we be aiming to make it easier to live as part of collectives and communities with a wider variety of bodily difference, by lowering the cost of medical treatments and expanding health-care access and other social services?"[50] Refusing individualized accommodations shifts the focus away from how my body, or yours, cannot digest certain substances and instead demands (and imagines) a space where all are welcome to partake of everything at the table.

A common refrain a food-allergic person might hear would be along these lines: if you need a nut-free baked good, then bake it yourself in your own kitchen, pay extra, plan in advance by purchasing something from a nut-free bakery (often in another city or state), or take a risk by eating something produced alongside other items containing your allergens. And this works for many allergic folks, especially those with varying degrees of racial, gender, and class privilege that allows their self-assessment to be believed and allows them to afford (or plan for) allergen-free goods. But many others take risks, their needs framed as unreasonable or beyond the scope of what can be expected. (As a contrast to Brandreth-Poynter's experience on GBBO, I am reminded of an episode of the U.S.-based competition cooking show *Chopped*. A contestant was allergic to one of the secret-basket ingredients but had to handle and cook with it anyway. In others, vegan or vegetarian contestants are expected to cook with ingredients they cannot taste or have no familiarity with.) I also have to note how it is more often than not white individuals (who sometimes also experience other levels of identity privilege, including gender, citizenship, and sexuality privileges) that are the ones whose stories of allergy success or tragedy are reported on.[51] With the exception of Kim-Joy Hewlett, the rest of the disabled contestants who have appeared on GBBO have been white.

I want to discuss another episode of GBBO, from season six. Episode five, "Free-From Week," required the contestant bakers to avoid certain ingredients— not because of allergy but to make the bakes more challenging. The opening bit asks viewers to imagine the food without its defining essence in British culture: including cake without sugar and bread with no gluten. Of course, this thought experiment will be resolved the following week, when sugar, wheat, and dairy will be back on the baking tables. Still, this episode and the series in general do not imagine that many people require sugar-free, gluten-free, and dairy-free food daily.

As Mannur remarks, "baking has a history in imperialism," and to bake a cake without sugar (or even molasses) asks the bakers to imagine a pantry from a preimperialist era.[52] But the opening round of the sugar-free competition, called the "signature challenge," does not talk about the exploitation connected to sugar, including enslavement and colonialism. Rather, substitutes such as honey, maple syrup, and agave are used to make carrot cakes, upside-down cakes, polenta cakes, and other items, and the judging mostly focuses on the right or wrong choices for fruit additions in the batter. For the second round of competition, the "technical challenge," the bakers are asked to make gluten-free pita breads using the recipe of one of the judges, Paul Hollywood. In the back and forth between Hollywood and another judge, Mary Berry, Berry remarks that many of the bakers probably have never baked with gluten-free flour before, and Hollywood says this version of the pita is almost as good as one with wheat flour. While mixing his dough, which includes psyllium powder, Tamal Ray proclaims, "This is rank." Indeed, many of the bakers wear looks of dismay as they struggle to make the dough workable. They struggle with kneading the sticky dough, the time required for proving, and even shaping the loaves. The final round of competition, "showstopper," involves the bakers making a dairy-free ice cream roll. Alvin Magallanes makes an ice cream roll using buko pandan, mango, and passion fruit, and explains to Berry, Hollywood, and Giedroyc that buko pandan, which is made from young coconut, is used in Southeast Asia in the same way that English recipes use vanilla. Hollywood remarks that the buko pandan "smells like sunscreen." This type of Western-centric aggressive reply from the judge works to construct Magallanes as "foreign" and not "British" in his ingredient selection. Nonwhite contestants are constantly questioned throughout the seasons by Hollywood, Berry, and

Leith for pushing the envelope with various spices and flavors. In this round, many of the bakers also use coconut and other "tropical" flavors, but it is only Magallanes that is questioned for his supposed sunscreen-smelling ingredients. (The winner of this episode, Hussain, is praised by Berry for masking coconut with chocolate ice cream.) The episode illustrates how allergies are framed as a challenge, deviant from the norm, and how supposedly "exotic" flavors like coconut need to be tamed or even masked by chocolate. Under the tent, white allergic bakers can be accommodated, but only in secret, if they don't require others to completely give up their nuts, dairy, eggs, and gluten.

I discuss these scenes to highlight various political, cultural, and legal dimensions of food allergy alongside more experiential considerations. Within disability communities, allergies might be trivialized, or assumed to not be disabling, and some with food allergies might not consider themselves disabled or as part of a group seeking to dismantle systems of oppression. Disability accommodations might not include the need to accommodate food allergies and other dietary needs. Foods provided in some spaces might not include ingredient lists or descriptions of potential cross-contamination. Likewise, food allergy activists might consider food allergy to be only a single-identity and single-experience concern, neglecting to attend to intragroup difference, especially around racial and class status, while also not considering how to join other groups of folks to advocate for coalitional responses to improve access to prescription drugs, food, and protections. In this text, I invite fellow individuals with food allergies to move beyond our important but limiting focus on schools, planes, and epinephrine to a more robust coalition that centers disabled people of color, and to consider how the same systems that those with food allergies navigate disproportionally affect BIPOC individuals, often resulting in adverse health outcomes and early, violent death.

Allergic Intimacies is an exploration of key debates about risks, dangers, safety, representations, and political concerns regarding the lives of food-allergic individuals. While this is a text that embraces, expands, and intervenes in disability studies, the work I cite and consider crosses disciplines and boundaries. I am making an explicit argument that what counts as disability theory should expand beyond a disability-only discussion. Writings that engage with intersectional lived experiences of illness/conditions, including allergies, are often more applicable to the day-to-day negotiations food-allergic individuals make. The whiteness of the food allergy community and of those who espouse single-identity disability theory is inherently limiting and insufficient to address the complex choices that those with food allergies make. Allergic calculations therefore go beyond calculations regarding safety but include calculations regarding identities. In what follows, I do address key disability studies concerns, including those of embodiment, what counts as disability, and how we should avoid addressing disability as a single-identity issue, all of which help to further contextualize my argumentation in the book. I discuss important issues regarding access to testing and treatment. I talk about the politics of creating peanut-free (and/or nut-free) spaces, especially in schools and airplanes (Chapter 1). I analyze the representation of food allergy in children's books (Chapter 2). I pay attention to how allergic people make decisions regarding dating and managing activities where allergens can be transmitted via fluids, most often saliva and semen (Chapter 3). Finally, I explore the continuum between accidental ingestion (which leads to multiple deaths a year) by individuals that purposely seek out food that is risky (because it might contain or does contain an allergen) and what deaths are mourned and what deaths are not (Chapter 4). Throughout all these case studies, I utilize the allergic calculation to determine how allergic individuals make choices balancing risk—both felt and perceived—with a desire to be spontaneous, safe, and partake in pleasurable moments.

I join Emily Brown and her fellow panelists at the 2020 Food Equality Initiative webinar—Karen Palmer, Lakiea Wright, Denise Woodard, Thomas and Dina Silvera, Javier Evelyn, and Linsey Davis—to highlight how much work needs to happen to shift the focus from a white allergic experience to one that is more representative of the racial and ethnic diversity of the United States. As Brown remarked, "representation matters";[53] the work by these Black leaders in allergy activism continues to demand that racism and structural violence are addressed and rectified to create more equitable spaces.

1
Relational Food Allergy, Immunity, and Environments

Our home was like a safe haven. We always wanted it to be. My kids can eat anything in my house. We don't buy anything with nuts in it. I always tell my husband, you have to eat it at work, triple wash your hands. Brush your teeth. We don't allow the tooth brush to even stay in the house. I throw it away, because it could have residue.

PARTICIPANT #23, FROM "'EVERYBODY ELSE GOT TO HAVE
THIS COOKIE': THE EFFECTS OF FOOD ALLERGEN
LABELS ON THE WELL-BEING OF CANADIANS"

Participant #23's experiences illustrate how individual actions affect others.[1] A husband eating nuts has the potential to go beyond an individual and the act of eating. Additionally, the quote helps to illuminate the relationship, explored in this chapter, between discourses of risk, safety, and environments. Notice in particular the use of "safe" and "residue" in the above statement. When an individual's dietary practices—due to allergy, religious practice (for example, halal or kosher), political and ethical practice/desire (vegetarianism/veganism), or personal preference—depend on another's actions or environments, what (if any) is the responsibility between the two individuals to meet the diverse dietary needs of each other? If you are allergic to eggs and go out to breakfast with a friend, should you also expect that friend to avoid eggs when ordering food? How can individuals make decisions when another's actions can result in compromised levels of safety? Or increased risk?

To address these questions, in this chapter I explore a disability studies approach to eating and accommodation, examining how interdependence and relationality affect individual food choices and eating habits. Susan Wendell writes that upholding notions of independence, particularly in disability rights movements, "tends to diminish the esteem of people who cannot live without a great deal of help from others, and to ignore or undervalue relationships of dependence or interdependence." Wendell continues, "If everyone with a disability is to be integrated fully into my society, without being 'the Other' who symbolizes moral failure, then social ideals must change in the direction of acknowledging the realities of our interdependence and the value of depending on others and being depended upon."[2] I am interested in extending Wendell's feminist disability analysis unto the politics of food and eating, especially as it relates to food allergies. In doing so, I argue that a disability studies approach to eating and accommodation shifts the focus from the individual to people in relationship with each other. As such, the person with specific dietary needs, for example, is not the only one requiring a certain meal. Instead, the entire dining party demands halal/kosher/vegan or allergen-free meals in order to destabilize an individualized approach to accommodations, allowing for creative and flexible modes of spontaneity and relationality.

In the chapter's three parts, I explore discourses of safety, risk, and identity claims surrounding food allergy; the politics around peanut bans and food allergy disability accommodations; and the potential to enact an ethic of accommodation to explore a disability studies approach to eating and accommodation. By focusing on how individuals with and without food allergies have temporal relationships to environments, including toxins (allergens) and other beings, discourses of safety and risk are destabilized, as are claims of identity to focus on how minority groups can disidentify to claim coalition. I also discuss how food allergy identity claims can reinforce white subjects as the only ones needing accommodation. In this chapter, I argue for a more coalitional approach that decenters individual claims of allergy toward a more relational model that facilitates more diverse and radical ways of being in community.

Part One: Thinking Through Safety and Risk

I often deal with calculations of risk. I also often deal with calculations of safety. These calculations are endlessly tied to notions of social acceptability and decorum. At various times, I have felt that I needed to embrace a high level of risk because I could not demand or afford safety. I recognize that I am being vague in discussing the intersection—or relationship—between risk and safety. I seek clear answers but often fail to find them. Even when I thought I was being safe, I faced a high level of risk. I also frequently wonder what gets lost in choosing safety over risk. What experiences, even if just temporary, am I missing? What new tastes and experiences am I unable to encounter? At what point do multiple engagements with risk outweigh a lifetime of safety? Am I living to avoid risk in the name of being safe?

In order to ground this discussion of risk and safety, I want to think about the foods we eat—perhaps breakfast this morning or a snack last night before bed. Think about our various motivations for choosing specific foods. As Marion Nestle argues, the food industry—through lobbying, target marketing, and public service campaigns, often funded with government assistance—have been encouraging Americans to "eat more." Our eating decisions are framed as personal, through the discourse of choice and taste, but they are also completely political. Nettle writes, "When food is plentiful and people can afford to buy it, basic biological needs become less compelling, and the principal determinant of food choice is personal preference. In turn, personal preferences may be influenced by religion and other cultural factors, as well as by considerations of convenience, price, and nutritional value."[3] Perhaps we are trying to avoid spending too much money, and so we consume something that is relatively low cost. We might be more concerned with convenience, prompting us to eat whatever is easily accessible. Our motivation is also nutritional—a desire to eat something that provides protein or fiber, is low in fat or sodium, or can be delivered via a feeding tube. Perhaps we want to avoid animal products because we are vegetarian or vegan. Perhaps our religious practice dictates certain foods as clean or acceptable to eat. If we are incarcerated in a prison or institution, we most likely have no choice over what is served for meals. Maybe the grocery stores we have access to do not carry ingredients that can be used to cook the food we grew up with. Maybe others consider the food we eat to be smelly, so we take a different lunch to work. Perhaps the restaurants near us do not accommodate our race and ethnicity, so we avoid eating out, or we only get food to go. We may eat to be accepted and included, even welcomed at the table. Sometimes we are most concerned with taste and satisfaction—we crave a slice of cheese pizza, a scoop of ice cream, a grilled steak, a ripe peach, toasted seaweed and rice, or a handful of cashews. Our motivation for what we eat changes based on our circumstances and surroundings. Sometimes we might eat for pleasure, while at other times we eat primarily for energy. These two motivations are not mutually exclusive. Material concerns and access to food are particularly important to underscore in thinking about our various food choices.[4] Residence in a food desert, or a location where unprocessed foods like vegetables and fruits are not easily accessible, limits options to purchase and consume diverse foods. Limited resources make prioritizing cheaper, subsidized food more efficient to meet nutritional needs, especially if we have to feed a large family or group of individuals. Cuts to public support in the name of austerity further tighten food budgets, while politicians and pundits seek to monitor what food is purchased by individuals using government assistance. Sparse public transportation, which might also be inaccessible to disabled individuals, affects access to various foods, as does the built space of the grocery store, market, restaurant, or cart where the food is purchased.

Thinking about the various foods I consume, one question I consider is whether the food contains nuts. On some level, this answer is a clear yes or no. The food either is a nut or contains nut-based products. But even if the meal is ostensibly nut free, how can I be sure? Chances are, unless the person consuming the meal has an allergy to nuts, it might not matter whether the meal came into contact with nuts or nut products, including nut oils and essences. If I eat a nut, my body will go into anaphylactic shock and release histamine, my throat will rapidly close, and at some point I will suffocate to death. My blood pressure may drop dramatically, my heart will race, and I might become unconscious before dying. Here is where the calculations of risk and safety are most salient. Am I taking a risk in eating certain foods? How can I know that a food is safe for me to eat? How close is the hospital? Will my insurance cover an out-of-town emergency room visit? When eating out with friends, how do I negotiate the desire to share a meal while trying to remain safe? Because of my severe allergies to tree nuts, I carry self-injectable epinephrine most of the time, although it is inevitable that I forget to carry it sometimes. If I accidentally eat a tree nut, I can inject the expensive prescription drug into my thigh to temporarily cease the progression of anaphylaxis before heading to an emergency room for steroid injections and medical follow-up. My multiple brushes with death via accidental ingestion of nuts are fairly mundane: cross-contamination at a restaurant, not realizing there was pesto on a pizza, eating a cookie that was made for me and thus supposedly "safe." In fact, I rarely, if ever, choose risk over safety, but I have inadvertently consumed nuts when I thought I was being safe. The relationship between safety and risk remains cloudy and confusing.

The production practices of the food manufacturer or the sanitization practices of the restaurant kitchen are important to consider. Allergen warnings on packages might be glanced over; phrases like "may contain" or "processed in a plant" do not seem to affect purchasing patterns. Bonnie Chow explains that the wide variety of allergen warnings leaves "consumers confused about the potential risks associated with consumption." Chow contends, "An individual's social construction of the illness and consumption risks, as shaped by the personal experiences of the allergy, guides their decision to consume or avoid products labeled with allergen warnings." An informant in a study conducted by Johan Fischer remarks, "There are times when you don't know if it is *halal* or not so you just say a Muslim prayer before you eat."[5] Consistent and reliable food labeling and certification are essential for all consumers—including those that practice halal, kosher, or vegan eating—for a variety of reasons. Despite the overuse of allergen warnings to mitigate producer liability and risk, establishing the trustworthiness of food labeling is a question that has life and death ramifications.

Of course, I know exactly how I can remain "safe" in relation to my nut allergy: avoid any foods, restaurants, or situations where nuts might be present. I could, for example, consume only food that I have cooked using ingredients that are unprocessed and free of allergens. I could eat in one of the very few restaurants that are free of nuts. Or I could purchase and consume only allergen-free products. In the last decade, many more companies have begun producing processed food items that are made in facilities that are free of various allergens. If I can access (and afford) these products—mostly processed snacks, mixes, and confectionaries—I can consume them while feeling at ease. Such products are usually two to three times more expensive then the regularly produced alternatives; thus, choosing them is a financial investment. When I depended on governmental food assistance, it was difficult to always choose safety over risk. The ability to be "safe" is not cheap. It might be impossible to be safe from allergens and to consume a nutritionally rich diet on a limited income, especially if the food budget is heavily supplemented by decreasing public assistance. I also regularly get notices from companies that are recalling items because of the presence of allergens not listed on the ingredient label, through either oversight or production error.

I do, however, find a unique sense of pleasure in consuming an allergen-free chocolate bar or sunflower-butter cup, knowing that these products will not trigger an allergic reaction. As many disability studies scholars have illustrated, a desire to feel "normal" is quite compelling but largely unattainable. Even as we live under the pressure of compulsory able-bodiedness, most of us fail to inhabit the ideal. I, for instance, appear to be able-bodied. My allergy to nuts is not always disabling, but I am aware that it is chronic, and I depend on medical technology (the medical model), access to health care (specifically, my injectable epinephrine and having a hospital nearby), the behaviors of others, and the availability of food to feel safe even when taking risks. And if I didn't take as many risks as I do, like eating in restaurants that have nuts in the kitchen, or flying on airlines that refuse to stop serving nuts, my allergy would limit my opportunities and access to social spaces. I need accessible and affordable emergency care and dependable portable medical technology to live if I consume a nut.

Yet I also find pleasure in consuming certain foods that are riskier because of the potential for cross-contamination. Some of my favorite foods and dishes are produced in restaurant kitchens (or market stalls) populated with nuts. In these moments, I balance risk and safety against pleasure and the reward of culinary satisfaction. If I were to exclusively choose safety—in foods, the company I keep, and restaurants—my options would be significantly limited. I might end up drinking water while watching my dining companions enjoy their meals, making them quite uncomfortable. Motivations for choosing risk include companionship, spontaneity, and pleasure. Quite frankly, I want to be a good guest that others want to be around.

Beyond food allergies, strategies for remaining connected with others while managing dietary restrictions or certain eating practices include determining what is "safe" or "allowable" to eat. Johan Fischer, Gabriele Marranci, Kamaludeen Mohamed Nasir, and Alexius Pereira all explore how Muslims in London and Singapore negotiate following halal dining practices in spaces heavily populated by nonhalal, unclean (haram) food options. Nasir and Pereira describe "defensive dining" as a practice that Muslims deploy in multicultural settings in Singapore, "a strategy utilized by individuals to maintain purity in an impure setting." It includes paying attention to unclean food and aromas, not touching surfaces that might be unclean, and "establishing a safe distance" from haram food in order to prevent contamination.[6]

Marranci complicates defensive dining practices by reporting on additional strategies deployed in Singapore by Malay Muslims, including bringing personal food to a party, refusing to shake hands, even among the same gender, because of fear of contamination, and refusing to drink from glasses in non-Muslim homes. Marranci reports how non-Muslims can become "unclean" "as a cause of contamination," because "halal food represents more than religious obligation" in Singapore, where Muslims are majority and non-Muslims are minority and have lower socioeconomic status. As such, halal food "is transformed into an 'act' of identity, a marker which allows not only a fully controlled space, but also an emotional one. . . . Halal food remains the only sphere in which the Malay Muslims are fully in control and the state— as well as other ethnic groups—are required to accommodate the minority's requests."[7]

The parallels between food allergy and religious observance are striking, especially in relation to the dependence on others (to ensure the purity of food without the allergens or unclean substances present) and the necessity for clear labeling of food. Islamophobia is a killing force, and consuming haram food can be considered a sin or poison requiring emergency care, including stomach pumping. These points are important to underscore in order to resist a simple comparison between food allergy and halal eating practices, despite the necessity for all types of eaters to be able to benefit from robust labeling practices and the availability of safe food. I bring up these connections to highlight how an ethic of accommodation around eating and being in community can extend beyond impairment-focused views of allergies to a broader understanding of community.

I practice "defensive dining" when in the presence of allergens. When someone eating nuts touches a piece of paper or a table I am using, I often make the automatic connection in my mind that the surface or item has become unclean. Yet I often fail to ask the individual not to eat nuts in my presence. Even when they ask me if it is okay to eat nuts, I pass at the chance to say anything but "Sure." It is challenging to assert my needs when I feel like I am inconveniencing another. Social notions of culture and class-specific decorum also affect my understanding of the relationship between risk and safety, as do expectations of masculine gender performance. When I receive a dinner invitation, I wonder how I should communicate my allergies. What I usually say to the host is that I am allergic to tree nuts. What I probably should communicate is something like this:

> Dear friend, Thank you for the invitation to dinner. As you might know, I am allergic to tree nuts. My allergy to tree nuts is life threatening, meaning that if I consume even a trace of a tree nut, my body will go into anaphylactic shock, and I will need to go to the emergency room to receive treatment. I carry self-injectable epinephrine with me at all times in case I consume a tree nut. My allergy is so severe that I should avoid products produced in a factory or environment where there is a risk of cross-contamination. Statements like "may contain" or "produced in a factory where nuts are present" means that the safety of that product is not certain. Sanitizing practices are essential in making sure that the cutting boards, utensils, and other implements of cooking are free from traces of nuts. Many allergens are found in various oils, extracts, and processed foods. Please let me know if my dietary concerns are too limiting. I am happy to work with you to find a solution to meet my needs.

In an effort to communicate the severity of my allergy and the risk of a potential reaction, I might alienate the host by appearing to question their cleaning and cooking practices. Halal and kosher eating requests might also communicate distrust toward a host who doesn't share the same practices. While it might appear impractical, or at least less important, to consider the needs and feelings of my host, I wonder how cultural customs tied to middle-class assumptions influence my typical decision to merely say that I'm allergic to tree nuts rather than communicating the longer and more accurate statement. The allergic calculation in this setting means I often do not share my full reality so that I can fit in with others and their expectations of me. The longer I go without an allergic reaction, the more risks I find myself taking, and the less consistent I am in my disclosure practices.

Here is the challenge: As a disability studies scholar committed to universal access and accommodations, I nevertheless fail to accurately express my allergy so I can avoid the risk of offending the host. Yet by doing so I jeopardize my safety for the sake of decorum and sociability. I individualize my accommodation needs, aligning my embodiment with the medical model's expectations. As a result I have found myself unable to trust various hosts when they assure me that the food they have prepared is nut free. I pop an antihistamine pill, which can help control an allergic reaction, inspect each bite of food, and hope for the best. As I flirt with risk, I feel less safe. I find myself wondering what the relationship is between individual bodies, allergens (or toxins that impose danger to everyone), and notions of interdependence. As someone with food allergies, I wonder what my responsibility is to ensure that my eating (as well as my cooking and cleaning) practices are welcoming to diverse bodies— those of individuals with disabilities, differing needs, religious practices, or eating preferences. Is anyone ever free from the presence of allergens? How can I enact a disability politics of food independent of discourses on individual safety and risk?

Part Two: Peanut Bans and Environmental Concerns

In March 2011, a small community in Florida became embroiled in a discussion around parental rights because of a food allergy disability accommodation. At the center of the controversy was an unnamed first-grade student at Edgewater Elementary School with a life-threatening peanut allergy. When parents of other children in the class demanded that the girl with allergies be homeschooled, the school district defended its position and the child's right to be in the classroom by invoking the Americans with Disabilities Act (ADA). (In some cases, parents of children with food allergies file 504 plans, which are separate from the ADA, to make sure their child's allergy is accommodated throughout the school day. Both approaches are used by parents to make sure their children's food allergies are accommodated in school.) The school-generated allergy accommodation plan included a complete ban on peanuts and products containing peanuts, a move similar to one adopted at school districts throughout the United States. It also mandated that all students in the allergic girl's classroom wash their hands at the beginning of the day and after lunch. (Of course, the irony is that during the COVID pandemic, many schools began mandating that students wash their hands multiple times a day.) Additionally, students had to wash their faces after lunch with a wet cloth. Parents of the children in the classroom took to the streets, protesting that these accommodations stole instruction time from their children, ultimately harming their educational experience. Caught up in the protest was an erroneous claim that the children had to wipe their faces with bleach wipes; rather, the bleach wipes were used to clean the desks in the classroom. Of note, the spokeswoman for the school district was quoted as saying that the peanut-related accommodations "would be the same thing as putting a handicap [sic] ramp for a student that is physically disabled. The only difference with this is that it affects other students."[8]

I am troubled by the claim that construes disability accommodation as primarily about the disabled individual, here the child with peanut allergies. In thinking through issues related to safety, risk, and environments, what would a crip approach to food allergies look like? Can a crip approach embrace diverse nutritional needs without isolating the individual with food allergies? Might the communal act of hand washing and face wiping as an "ethic of accommodation" foster what Muñoz calls "disidentification" to describe queer of color existence that "negotiate[s] a phobic majoritarian public sphere that continuously elides or punishes the existence of subjects who do not conform to the phantasm of normative citizenship"?[9] How can we crip notions of safety and risk to reveal ableist trends and presumptive able-bodied norms?

Legal statutes ensuring access for disabled people are increasingly being used to justify the banning of peanuts in certain locations, even though the bans are construed as infringing on the rights of others. For example, following the Edgewater ban parents were quoted as saying, "If I had a daughter who had a problem, I would not ask everyone else to change their lives to fit my life," and "We're talking about a peanut allergy, something that's individual to that kid. I don't think it's something that's contagious. I mean if we were talking about some type of contagious disease, yeah I can see that. But, [the ban] doesn't make any sense." Both quotes describe the food allergy as an individual concern, thus supposedly warranting an individual- (not group-) based accommodation. Transmissibility becomes a condition for the isolation of the infected. Matthew Smith highlights how peanut allergy is divisive because of "its ability to change public-health policy."[10]

Total peanut bans are controversial, as some consider them unnecessary. For example, Food Allergy Research and Education, a national organization in the United States, advocates educating teachers, administrators, parents, and fellow students on allergies and changing laws to allow schools to carry epinephrine shots in nurses' offices. In 2013, President Barack Obama signed the School Access to Emergency Epinephrine Act, which authorizes (but doesn't require) schools to carry emergency epinephrine and allow trained school staff to administer the shots to students. Part of the rationale for the legislation is that increasing numbers of school-age children have food allergies (5.6 million), and roughly 20 to 25 percent of all epinephrine injections occur following a reaction when a food allergy was not previously known about. On average, 150 to 200 children and adults die annually from food-related allergic reactions in the United States.[11] The bill sought to address these preventable deaths. It should be noted that many states have mandated schools to carry epinephrine, but not all schools are required to do so.

Nicolas Christakis problematically calls peanut bans in schools, with their attendant requirements for hand washing, a type of "mass psychogenic illness," known more colloquially as "epidemic hysteria." Christakis is generally skeptical of these bans and makes the claim that they are "making things worse" by signaling to parents that nuts are cause for concern. He argues that nut bans in schools further sensitize children to nuts, thus potentially causing more allergic reactions later because of the lack of exposure, creating "feedback loops [in which] the policy of avoidance ends up creating the epidemic it is trying to stop."[12] Christakis equates school policy that is often covered under federal disability rights legislation with a type of psychosis. Recall the earlier quote from the parent who made the statement about the difference between a contagious disease and an allergy to nuts and how it implies that the person with the allergy should become isolated; it is assumed they need to be dealt with individually. Most often the suggested course of action is either segregation (in separate tables at the lunchroom—all the allergic kids together) or isolation (advocating that the child be homeschooled). In the name of "safety," a disabled child is isolated. Segregation and isolation are all too familiar for many disabled people and people of color. Disabled people have long struggled for their rights to community integration as opposed to state-funded segregation in special education classrooms, nursing homes, and residential institutions, and placement in sheltered workshops and vocational rehabilitation programs. Discourses of segregation and contamination have been lodged at Black bodies, utilizing racism and white supremacy to insist on separate restaurants and culinary spaces. The forces of white supremacy and ableism are used to justify incarceration, institutionalization, and segregation.

Some food allergy advocates are using the disability rights term "least-restrictive environment" (LRE) to advocate for food-free classrooms to counter exclusionary practices and spaces. The trap in using the language of LRE is that the rationale for restrictions is not challenged. Instead of demanding removal of all barriers that prevent participation, LRE seeks to remove only some of the structures that increase segregation.

Discourses of risk and safety affect how environments become welcoming or prohibiting. Demanding classrooms (and camps, teams, and other locations) where *all* are welcome regardless of social location, including racial status and ability, gets us closer to actualizing disability justice dreams and goals.

Part Three: Toxins, Identity, Ethics, and Accommodation

In the documentary *Vital Signs: Crip Culture Talks Back*, white disability studies scholar Harlan Hahn explains disability culture and notes that cultures have foods associated with them. He points out that many in the disabled community obtain food from drive-through windows at fast-food restaurants. In his book *My Life in Institutions and My Way Out*, Michael Kennedy remarks that when he lived in the Rome State School, an institution for individuals with labels of intellectual and developmental disabilities, institutional staff would load residents in a van and pick up coffee through the McDonald's drive-through, calling it "community integration." Hahn's comment in the film and Kennedy's experience point to how institutionalization, incarceration, and exclusionary built environments prohibit individuals from accessing a multitude of community spaces. Describing the scene in *Vital Signs*, Kim Q. Hall writes, "Hahn recalls countless conversations with other disabled people and presents a wonderful moment of crip humor, full of sharp critique for a society that makes dining out an exercise in various forms of tiresome hoop-jumping for many disabled people."[13] Hahn is likely not speaking about people with certain food allergies but rather addressing the physical inaccessibility of restaurants. However, his remark about the drive-through window addresses the structural, social, and racial barriers that prohibit some disabled individuals of color, including those with certain food allergies, from partaking in a meal with others, especially when the restaurant space is racist and hostile.

In the introduction to a special issue of *Disability Studies Quarterly* on disability and food, Elaine Gerber, who edited the issue, notes that disability studies has paid little attention to food and likewise has focused in only a limited way on "ways in which the social construction of food and eating may create disabling conditions and/or maintain disability boundaries or, for that matter, help to reduce and eliminate disabling and stigmatizing conditions." While the issue does not address what Gerber calls "food-related disorders," including food allergies, she does remark that these impairments "if severe enough, can prevent people from leaving the house or participating in food-related events. . . . People are financially and socially disadvantaged by an inability to 'break bread' together." In a more recent publication Gerber writes, "The dietary divide experienced by disabled people is central to perpetuating inequality based on bodily difference and reinforces stereotypes that harm disabled people; it is even implicated in sociocultural construction of disability itself."[14] Food insecurity, often due to racialized poverty, a lack of control over shopping and cooking, and shrinking governmental food assistance, is deeply tied with ableist oppressions. Coalitions that address the problems of food production—including monocrops, use of antibiotics and pesticides, labor exploitation of workers of color, including disabled workers of color, and food insecurity exacerbated by racism and settler colonialism—should be central concerns of a crip agenda.

As a way to theorize a disability studies approach to eating and food, and to begin to understand the relationship between safety, risk, and environments, I want to revisit the accommodation plan at Florida's Edgewater Elementary School and put it in conversation with disability studies work on accommodation, ethics, toxicity, and disability identity. Imagine twenty to thirty first-grade children lined up to wash their hands and faces to ensure a safe and allergen-free space for their classmate. In these moments of communal washing (and removal of toxins, to invoke Mel Y. Chen's theorizations), the children are developing a ritual that by extension welcomes the child with the impairment; by refusing peanuts, the children are enacting an ethic of accommodation that destabilizes the boundaries around allergies, disability, safety, risk, and inclusion.[15]

In discussing theatre and inclusion, Terry Galloway, Donna Marie Nudd, and Carrie Sandahl describe the ethic of accommodation as "a particular practice of inclusion that does not simply issue an invitation to everyone to participate in theatre-making. Equal treatment does not always translate into equal opportunity. Genuine inclusiveness requires a willingness to make changes to core beliefs, practices and aesthetics."[16] True inclusion and accommodation accordingly demand a reexamination of the core of any activity or setting. Creating classroom policies requires consideration of which bodies and experiences are excluded through the day-to-day practices. How are some bodies never legitimatized because of exclusion? And which exclusions are not recognized as such?

I am struck with how the act of communal washing for the sake of welcoming diverse bodies with distinct needs constitutes a type of accommodation that questions the need to isolate or exclude, even redress. Earlier, I quoted an administrator at Edgewater School who likened the peanut allergen policy with that of constructing a ramp. Both accommodations attempt to ensure access. The administrator noted that the peanut policy was different from the ramp in that it affects other students. Certainly, this is a somewhat narrow articulation of the scope of building a ramp (or changing physical environments) by assuming that only the individual requiring a ramp would access that space. Additionally, considering the ramp as constructed for individual disabled students fails to address the relational or affective outcome of such a modification. Unlike the administrator's claim, both accommodations affect other students insomuch as each individual student becomes a part of the microcosm of the school and classroom. And because of this connectivity, the ethic of accommodation challenges a deficit model of access that seeks to ensure only participation as opposed to reciprocal interaction and commitment. But beyond the collectivity that these accommodations can foster, there is a potential to also foster an identification with those whom these interventions target.

In the introduction to *Sex and Disability*, Robert McRuer and Anna Mollow highlight "the risk of reifying identity categories that might be better contested." Both Mollow and McRuer negotiate the process of "coming out," to use Ellen J. Samuel's phraseology, of disclosing or claiming disability status, of making visible again what might be rendered invisible. They contend that identity claims have the potential to exclude, while also being judged as not authentic. Citing Samuels, they discuss how the complicated negotiation and potential exclusions of identity can have material effects in regard to accommodations, particularly accommodations that are interpreted as being "widely unreasonable" or "impossible." Peanut bans as accommodation are often construed as unreasonable and interpreted as infringing on the rights of the majority, who are assumed to be nondisabled. Even suggesting peanut bans or restrictions of nuts for access and inclusion brings forth calls for segregation and isolation of the allergic children for the sake of the nonallergic. Despite the assumption that the population of children with food allergies is small, a recent comprehensive frequency study determined that 8 percent of children in the United States have food allergies, a significantly higher number than previously estimated.[17]

An example of how identity claims are deployed to create awareness can be seen in a campaign the Arizona Food Allergy Alliance utilized for Food Allergy Awareness Week 2012 (May 13–19). The alliance released a series of advertisements on Facebook meant to "create education and awareness surrounding food allergies." The advertisements appeared in both English and

Spanish and featured short educational messages about allergies, such as warnings about cross-contamination and reminders to carry autoinjector epinephrine. The first shows a young white girl, maybe three to four years of age, with
shoulder-length blonde hair, leaning on a counter. One arm is lying on top of
the counter, the other is supporting her face, with her hand covering her chin
and mouth. She is looking directly into the camera. Next to the girl, in block
white letters, are the following words: "Exclude the food, not the child." The
next image shows four children, all white, three boys, one girl. They are most
likely four or five years old. They are lying on green grass; their elbows are
planted in the grass and their hands are framing their faces. Below the children
appears the following: "Which one of us has a food allergy? You can't see my
disability, but it doesn't make it any less real." The first image of the young
girl addresses issues of exclusion. In doing so, the advertisement aims to generate feelings of sympathy. Whiteness is problematically used in the advertisements to garner awareness and sympathy while reinforcing structural racism
within food allergy communities and the assumption of white children as needing intervention. The open letter from Emily Brown, referenced in the Preface, was written nine years after this campaign. The overall whiteness of the
food allergy community, both in advocacy and representation, illustrates how
class- and race-based privilege continues to operate in the ability to purchase
"safe" food, receive allergy testing and diagnosis, be seen as experts, and find
a sympathetic audience for claims of exclusion. Some (white) children are seen
as vulnerable to risk and need to be made safe, while other children are not
even called into being. White supremacy needs to be challenged in relation
to the framing and discussion of food allergy. Which bodies are excluded, and
which exclusions are not registered as such? How are food allergies construed
as a white, Western, upper- to middle-class issue? The other image addresses
visibility. The four children in the image described above are subject to the
test of visibility, the "diagnostic gaze."[18] There is no way to tell which child
has food allergies. Of interest is the last line of the advertisement, voiced by
the child with the allergies: "You can't see my disability, but it doesn't make it
any less real." The "you" in the ad is addressed by invoking an ocular ethic of
invisibility. Additionally, the "realness" of the quote calls for inclusion into the
category of disability, a claim that seems to work counter to the identity theorization articulated by McRuer and Mollow. Essentially, the ad calls for an understanding of disability regardless of preconceived notions of visibility. The
process of claiming, despite invisibility—for we do not know which of the four
children is voicing the claim—renders the category of food allergies variable.
Ability is also rendered invisible. Is there a crip potential for these children
with food allergies, a crip politics of food? How can we dismantle systems of

exclusion to foster collectivity between minority subjects to imagine crip spaces where bodies are not excluded? How can we continue to destabilize claims of legitimacy, which are made using white privilege, so knowledge about bodies is taken as truth regardless of diagnosis or documentation?

In part one of this chapter, I gestured toward my relationship between illness (medical condition writ large), disability, and identity claims. The relationship between safety and risk, visibility, and experiences of exclusion and oppression are also configured, often convolutedly, in any personal understanding of identity. In addition, remaining free from allergic reaction often depends on the actions of another, including workers in food factories, chefs, and friends. In line with Alison Kafer, Robert McRuer, and Carrie Sandahl, my contemplation around issues of identity and disability is a commitment that what counts as, can be claimed as, or inhabits the category of disability ought to be contested. I am thinking of my relationship between allergy and disability *and* impairment to consider how my relationship to these—seemingly stable but inherently messy—categories changes and shifts. As an example, when I enter a space, be it a restaurant, a home, or a country, where nut-based products are widely used, the registers of allergy and impairment are activated. When I acknowledge the presence of allergens, or the potential for an allergic reaction, my relationship between my body and impairment resurfaces in my perception of the surroundings. In the "safety" of my home, I reorient my understanding of my body and allergies. My temporal relationship to my surroundings, including environments, people, and objects (nuts and otherwise), shifts to change registers of time and space.[19] As I claim my allergies and desire access to medical care and technology, my own experience of embodiment is dependent on the needs, actions, and desires of others. Perhaps my own experience of allergies—and desire for allergen-free spaces—casts out others, even if unknowingly.[20] I desire a coalition and assemblage of diverse bodies, with various relationships and dependencies on environments, working together.[21]

I find myself wondering how individual bodies, dependent on each other but also on seemingly inanimate matter (for me, nut dust and particles), negotiate the meeting of intercorporeality not tied to discourses of agency and sentience. As I enter a space, how can my bodily needs be communicated and addressed? As I depend on others to not transfer allergens on clothing, hands, food, in saliva, how does the shifting dynamic environment welcome crip, queer, disabled, nonwhite, and otherwise excluded bodies?

Mia Mingus describes "access intimacy" as "the elusive, hard to describe feeling when someone else 'gets' your access needs." Mingus continues, "The kind of eerie comfort that your disabled self feels with someone on a purely access level. Sometimes it can happen with complete strangers, disabled or not, or sometimes it can be built over years. It could also be the way your body relaxes and opens up with someone when all your access needs are being met." I find myself dwelling on the possibilities of this intimacy as a mode of shifting from exclusion to inclusion, of blurring identity claims and claims of crip. In meeting the needs or requirements of another, interpersonal intimacy fosters inclusion and interdependence, an ethic of accommodation. Mingus writes how access intimacy is "hard won, organic or at times even magical" while also being "exciting and relieving, like a long slow exhale." Mingus remarks, "Access intimacy is something I am coming to understand that I need in my life; something that I cannot (and don't want to) live without. I need it to literally be my whole self because access is such an intimate part of my life as a queer physically disabled woman of color adoptee."[22] Access intimacy is vitally important to sustain and maintain, especially because of interlocking systems of oppression.

In thinking about Mingus's framing, I, too, remember individuals who, after I communicated my access needs, got it and continue to get it. I can interact with them over a meal and not feel concerned or excluded. When an individual lets me know that they read labels or inquired about sanitization practices on my behalf, I am surprised but also delighted that they have remembered, acknowledged, and *incorporated* my allergy. They are cripping my allergy, destabilizing identity and access claims, for the sake of inclusion and mutuality. This is also part of the allergic calculation. While this topic is outside the scope of the chapter, I see the relevance and importance of how such an approach for nut allergies (and accommodations) could be extended to other food- and drink-related matters, including choosing to not eat meat in the presence of a vegetarian, ensuring halal or kosher regulations, or withholding consumption of alcohol in the presence of an alcoholic. Beyond issues of consumption of beverages and food, crip identification can foster inclusivity for individuals with multiple chemical sensitivity and other impairments that are dependent on environmental factors. Alison Kafer discusses the importance of an "expansive disability movement" that can "trace the ways in which we have been forged as a group" while tracing "the ways in which those forgings have been incomplete, or contested, or refused." These forgings have been (and continue to be) "inflected by histories of race, gender, sexuality, class, and nation."[23] The taking of whiteness as the default subject, the focus on the physical body, and the Euro-American experiences of the archive of disability studies and manifestations of group formations can be cripped to expand understandings of identity, interdependence, (inter)corporeality, and relationships between individuals and environments.

In thinking again about safety and risk, I don't find myself wanting to eat nuts, or even wanting a cure for my allergies. I suppose my lack of desire to eat nuts is connected to seeing pecans, pine nuts, and their relatives as lethal. Even if I were cured of my allergies, it would be hard to sit down to a meal of pesto pasta, given that previously the same meal could have been my last. If a cure were available, we would need to ensure that the cure was available to all. Even with cures, though, the need for various accommodations for certain eating practices will continue. If I were cured of my allergy, I don't know if I would ever enjoy (or even seek out) a meal with nuts. Once a food product becomes lethal or toxic, I expect it would be hard to reclaim that product as pleasurable or even desirable. Can nuts ever become safe given their current status as risky? The taste and smell can certainly trigger a psychosomatic response, even if the individual is "safe."[24] When I smell roasted nuts, for example, I feel my throat tingle, but is the throat tingling because of aerosolized proteins, or because the smell reminds my body of previous reactions when I consumed nuts and required a trip to the emergency room? In thinking about issues related to future and temporality, I don't envision a future me as a nut eater. I do, however, imagine and desire a future where a politics of food expands conceptions of livability. Where communities and assemblages become intentional spaces fostering inclusivity, an inclusivity that is not tied to productivity, but rather acknowledges and appreciates multiplicities of beings, environments, identifications.

Mel Y. Chen theorizes "toxic animacies" and how chemicals or toxics more broadly are animate, thus illustrating "a potency and intensity to two animate or inanimate bodies passing one another, bodies that have an exchange—a potential queer exchange . . . that effectively risks implantation of injury." Chen continues: "The quality of the exchange may be at the molecular level, where airborne molecules enter the breathing apparatus, molecules that may or may not have violent bodily effects, or the exchange may be visual, where the meeting of eyes unleashes a series of pleasurable or unpleasurable bodily reactions such as chill, pulse rush, adrenaline, heat, fear, tingling skin." Thinking of food allergies in the context of Chen's assertion illustrates the animate potential of peanut dust and the rationale behind the communal hand washing at Edgewater Elementary. The invisibility of the toxin, which could trigger an allergic reaction, is addressed by the communal action, potentially rendering the toxin and impairment irrelevant, therefore dissolved. I follow Chen's formulation by applying it to my own experience. "Standing before you, I ingest you. There is nothing fanciful about this. I am ingesting the nut particles on your clothes, the nut oil in your lotion, lip balm, soap, shampoo, and makeup."[25] Nut toxins can be all around. We ingest parts of each other, the environment, and objects on a continual basis. Skin cells, perfume, peanut dust, car exhaust, and saliva are but a few of the potential toxins consumed in an afternoon. Toxins can cause impairment, disable, and even quicken death. Risk, safety, and the allergic calculation reemerge.

As a way to conclude, I want to return to the classroom full of children, some with allergies—to dairy, gluten, shellfish, peanuts, tree nuts, smoke, pollen, chemicals—and some without documented allergies. These two groups of children, without visible markers of allergens, are nevertheless tied unequally to the presence or absence of toxins—or allergens. What responsibility does one group have toward the other? The advertisements from the Arizona Food Allergy Alliance—in particular the one resisting classification based on visuality—transpose the relationship between allergen (toxin) and individual to a relational model of accommodation addressing the animate allergen and thus destabilizing identity.

Through enabling a type of independency, the needs of one are taken up by many. This type of sharing results in shifting the responsibility from one to multiple, meaning that the allergic (or intolerant, or vegan, or alcohol avoidant, etc.) are not the only ones needing the "special" cookies (or drinks) placed at the end of the table. Think of the implications when your lunch is packaged separately from others' lunches and consists of unappetizing, premade cold food. Rather, imagine that the entire table or menu or event has been planned to ensure that all dietary/nutritional/eating practices are met, with choice, pleasure, and taste in mind. Access intimacy focuses on meeting each other's needs as a type of interpersonal connection. Crip identification converges on the process of becoming, or alliance, or identifying with, or joining or remaining in communion. In these moments of communality, an ethic of accommodation emerges, enacting a crip approach to eating and food.

2

Nut-Free Squirrels and Princesses with Peanut Allergies

Food Allergies, Identity, and Children's Books

In *The Day I Met the Nuts*, an unnamed white boy has an allergic reaction at a friend's birthday party after eating two bites of "double chocolate muddy-nutty cake." Almost immediately he remarks, "The Nuts attacked me like wild fire ants. I itched and I scratched, and the madness made me quite mad." Later Dr. McFever tells the boy, "You + nuts = disaster." After this proclamation of disaster, the boy and his mother set off to make sure he successfully avoids The Nuts. *The Day I Met the Nuts* is one of many English-language children's picture books that address children's food allergies. They are often written with an audience in mind that includes both children with food allergies and nonallergic children who want to accommodate their food-allergic friends. *The Day I Met the Nuts* follows this trend with the following blurb on the back cover: "What would you do if YOU were allergic to The Nuts?"[1]

The reader follows the boy as he first becomes consumed with the belief that he will never eat any delicious chocolate again and that all his favorite foods contain nuts: "Nuts in breads. Nuts in pies. Nuts in salad dressing. Nuts hiding out in cereal. As if they couldn't just take a vacation and go someplace else." But the boy slowly adjusts to a life free of nuts, with help from his family and friends. At the grocery store, the boy meets a young boy of color who is allergic to bananas and an older white male cashier who is allergic to black-berries.[2] At school, the boy eats his lunch at the nut-free lunch table with some of his friends and other kids with allergies. They form a "NO NUTS ALLOWED club." The illustrations depict five children of various genders and racial categories holding signs that read, "NOT ONE MORE NUT!" "DOWN WITH

43

NUTS!" "HONK IF YOU'RE ALLERGIC TO NUTS!!" "HEY! HO! NUTS MUST GO!" "WE SAY NO!" "NO ROOM 4 NUTS!" Even the reluctant squirrel carries a sign: "OK, NO NUTS."

Borrowing from classic protest signs for social justice, the text shows the children advocating for themselves while forming a community around an identity, what Paul Rabinow refers to as "biosociality," defined as "a circulation network of identity terms and restrictions loci, around which and through which a truly new type of autoproduction" emerges.[3] Working within institutional constraints, including a segregated space in the cafeteria, the children form a club to support each other and their need for nut-free food (and spaces). The book highlights that membership in the club is not dependent on having an allergy, rather just on a commitment not to bring nuts to the space. The text closes with the boy assuring the reader that his adjustment to life with an allergy is complete: "The day I met The Nuts changed everything. I made new friends, have a cool club, and I can even read some big words now. The Nuts and I have agreed to stay away from each other. . . . Just me going NUT FREE! And I feel good." The penultimate illustration shows various nuts boarding a bus bound for Nutgonnaeatya Island. On the island there are peanuts in bikinis, pecans barbecuing, cashews swimming, and almonds playing in the sand.

The Day I Met the Nuts is like other picture books about allergies in that the narrative moves from a story of the individual (usually a young white boy) and their processes of diagnosis and developing strategies of avoidance to some larger supportive unit (most often a family and select group of friends, sometimes also with allergies of their own) engaging with the individual and supporting their new allergen-free life. In this chapter, I examine how allergies (and food sensitivities) are communicated to children, especially paying attention to the use of scientific understandings of immunity and reaction as communicable concepts for learners of various ages. I trace how discourses of safety and risk are deployed to communicate the necessity to avoid allergens while maintaining some freedom to make choices outside of parental purview. I also address the almost single-identity-focused representation of white children with food allergies, which reinforces the assumed whiteness of the overall food-allergic community in the West, despite epidemiological studies to the contrary.[4] I argue for a diversification of representation that moves beyond white homogeneous narratives of diagnosis and avoidance from parents who have the means to access medical care and alternative food choices, toward narratives of resilience that capture the ways children with food allergies navigate medical, educational, and social institutions.

Is Nut-Eating Essential to Squirrelness?

Nutley: The Nut-Free Squirrel begins with, "Hello! My name is Nutley. I know this may sound strange, but I'm a nut-free squirrel. I guess I should explain." Nutley brings friends together to discuss Nutley's allergy and create a plan to prevent future allergic reactions. Nutley recounts their experience of visiting a doctor and receiving the advice to avoid nuts and undergo regular allergy testing. Nutley, recalling the meeting with the friends, remarks, "A squirrel allergic to nuts—how odd! I thought I'd feel alone 'til one of my friends stood up and declared, 'I'm a dog allergic to bones!'"[5] Additional friends share their allergies, including a fly that cannot eat pitted fruit, a bee that is allergic to pollen, and a bird that is allergic to fish. The friends decide to keep each other "safe" by bringing nut-free treats (and presumably fish-free, pitted fruit–free, and pollen-free snacks) when they hang out.

As a plot device, portraying a squirrel that is allergic to nuts provides a cute hook to attract young readers. Of course, these tropes are well worn when imagining melodramatic stories of disability—for example, journalistic accounts of a one-handed pianist or a long-distance runner with one leg.[6] In an ableist imagination, having both hands or legs function "normally" is a precondition for the ability to play the piano or run. Thus, running with one leg or playing the piano with one hand seems to challenge the assumption of "normalcy," using an image of what Eli Clare refers to as the "supercrip": "Supercrip stories never focus on the conditions that make it so difficult for people with Downs to have romantic partners, for blind people to have adventures, for disabled kids to play sports. I don't mean medical conditions. I mean material, social, legal conditions. I mean lack of access, lack of employment, lack of education, lack of personal attendant services. I mean stereotypes and attitudes. I mean oppression. The dominant story about disability should be about ableism, not the inspirational supercrip crap, the believe-it-or-not disability story."[7] A children's book about food insecurity, or why Nutley can't access food other than nuts, might seem far-fetched, but what Clare and others are calling for is a representational politics that can simultaneously explore the lived embodiment of impairment while exposing systems of oppression and material conditions that assume disabled lives are only worth living when they are "super" extraordinary.

Is eating nuts essential to squirrelness? Does Nutley become something other than a squirrel because their favorite snacks are gummy bears, not acorns? Or rather, more to the point, is the ability to eat peanut butter sandwiches an essential quality of being a (white) child in the United States? Certainly, part of the goal of these picture books is to communicate that children with food allergies (most often to peanuts) can still have fun with friends, go to school, and eat foods like cookies and cake. On one level, then, the discourse is about expanding the notion of being a kid in this country beyond linking peanut butter consumption to discourses of normalcy.

At the risk of being too didactic and teleological, I will add that questions of nationalism are embedded in these choices of representation as well. Although the phrase "American as apple pie" is assumed to be a culinary marker denoting typicalness (and whiteness by virtue of the food's blonde color), Emily Upton discusses how apples can be traced to *Malus sieversii*, a wild apple native to Central Asia. In addition, the first "recorded recipe" for apple pie appeared in 1381 in England. During World War II, soldiers told journalists they were fighting for "motherhood and apple pie," which lead to the phrase "as American as motherhood and apple pie."[8] Apples were brought to the United States by colonialists. So on one level, apple pie is the perfect metaphor for the settler colonialist history of this country, where apples grown from imported seeds replaced crab apples—and Indigenous knowledge, and biodiversity. Instead, the Red Delicious apple or the Granny Smith becomes the representative apple, while other types are labeled wild. To claim apple pie as American, then, is to gloss over the ways in which the pastry is connected to the settler colonial history of the United States. There is nothing uniquely "American" about apple pie, yet nationalism becomes linked to the dish when the military machinery utilizes an imagined pie—and all it is assumed to represent— as justification for war.

Like the apple, the peanut, too, becomes a settler colonialist agricultural product, illuminating the ways in which white supremacy has been linked to culinary (and crop) valuation. The National Peanut Board, part of the U.S. Department of Agricultural Marketing Service and funded through commodity checkoff, on its "History of the Peanut" page states, "Africans were the first people to introduce peanuts to North America beginning in the 1700s."[9] Conveniently, the history of the peanut outlined here fails to mention the transatlantic slave trade and the material conditions that lead to enslaved Africans importing peanuts as a valuable source of nutrition. Andrew Smith writes about how peanuts were grown by enslaved peoples in this hemisphere: "In the Caribbean and in the British colonies in North America slaves grew peanuts on small garden plots given them by plantation masters. At the time, the white colonists do not appear to have consumed peanuts directly, but they did eat swine and poultry fattened on unlimited access to 'ground pease.'"[10]

It was not until the nineteenth century that peanuts were consumed as snacks in cities in the North. Smith writes, "Unlike other food fads that quickly passed from the culinary scene, peanuts thrived and eventually became enshrined as an American icon."[11] In a matter of centuries, the peanut (and the many products made with them) is transformed from an important crop grown for valuable nutrition by enslaved persons to something linked to national identity. The violent settler colonial history is erased when peanut butter sandwiches are assumed to be only quintessential lunches for (white) American school kids.

So, is Nutley less of a squirrel because they cannot eat nuts? Is the ability to eat nuts an essential activity linked to being a squirrel? Many children in the United States are raised eating peanut butter sandwiches. Perhaps the key point here is the *ability* to eat, not necessarily actually consuming, meaning if one is unable to eat certain foods then they are suspect. (Of course, many nonwhite children who might be first generation or who recently migrated to the United States experience discrimination and ostracization from their peers in school for their "weird" or "stinky" packed lunches. Smell is often code for "foreignness," while peanut butter and jelly sandwiches presumably are the quintessential lunch. Peanut butter has a distinct smell, but the ability to label some things as "smelly" and others as without scent is another marker of how white supremacy manifests in cafeterias and school lunch tables.) I am also reminded of the backlash that often occurs when peanuts are banned in schools, which I discussed in the previous chapter. The allergic child (or children) is usually isolated—and assumed to be the problem that needs to be removed from the school. Calls for homeschooling or segregating the child usually are expressed when the debate around peanut bans frames the majority as inconvenienced by the "needs" of the few.

Children with peanut allergies at school are a frequent topic of exploration in these children's books. For example, *Patty's Secret: A Tale of a Girl with Food Allergies* is about twin pigs, Patty and Patrick. Patty is nervous about how she will fit in with her allergy and prays for it to disappear before she starts school. At school, Patty eats a bite of a peanut butter cupcake and almost immediately develops a rash, hives, swollen eyes, other visible signs of an allergic reaction. Patrick gives Patty's injectable epinephrine shot to the teacher, Mrs. Zebra, who proceeds to give the shot to Patty in front of the class. Despite Patty's desire not to have her allergy known about, her secret is exposed to all through the visible signs of her reaction and the need for immediate medical intervention. The text ends with a lesson to Patty (and all) that allergies are not "a curse but a challenge," and she can "be healthy and safe as long as she didn't hide the truth."[12]

These texts attempt to communicate to children that their food allergies (or food sensitivities) need not negate their ability to have fun with their friends.

Woolfred Cannot Eat Dandelions is a "tale of being true to your tummy." Like Patty, Woolfred, a sheep, has a reaction after consuming a food he should not have. After he ate a large bunch of dandelions, "His mouth went dry. His belly was growing like a balloon. His legs went all wobbly. Thud. Down he went . . . and out came the dandelions." Woolfred knows he cannot eat dandelions, but he cannot stop thinking about them, partially because they are so delicious: "He knew what would happen if he ate them, but all Woolfred could think about was dandelions, dandelions, dandelions!" He tries to only eat part of the dandelion, but he has the same reactions. Ultimately he is separated from the flock as they go to play and Woolfred is weak from his reactions to the dandelions: "Weeks of eating dandelion parts had left Woolfred weak and tired. This time, when he hit the ground, he didn't get up. He lay there for a very long time in a restless sleep. When he finally woke up, it was to the sounds of the flock playing in the valley. He watched from the top of the hill as the rest of his friends frolicked together."

Woolfred is alone because he could not stop eating the forbidden plants. The message, of course, even if it is a bit heavy handed, is that not paying attention to your medical needs will prevent you from playing (or frolicking) with your friends. It is only when Woolfred focuses on his desire to play with his friends that he gives up the desire to eat dandelions and commits to changing his eating habits. Realizing that his friends in the flock all have unique characteristics, Woolfred races down the hill to catch up with the rest of the flock and runs past the dandelions. For example, his friend Franklin "secretly snacks on flies." Daisy has "no sense of direction." Bert "likes to scratch his bottom on the ground." And, of course, Woolfred "cannot eat dandelions." The message of the text is clear: all sheep have their quirks, and each makes the individual unique.[13]

Nutley, Patty, and Woolfred are all faced with challenges. The books highlight how they depend on others to support them in their journey to self-acceptance. In the note to parents and caregivers in the back of *Woolfred*, there is a mention to watch out for bullying, but the texts do not mention that any of the characters experience bullying from their friends. In fact, even though Woolfred is separated from the flock, the text emphasizes how others in the flock beg him to avoid eating dandelions so he can play with them. These three books and others encourage the readers, assumed to be children with food allergies or sensitivities, to accept their needs and be unafraid to communicate them to others—by wearing bracelets, having specially marked lunch boxes that indicate the necessity of avoiding certain foods, and carrying their medicine with them at all times. Nutley, Patty, and Woolfred are each able to find a supportive community to understand their dietary differences.

Yet the books do not illuminate the interpersonal negotiations the characters must engage in, especially if they are assumed to be "odd" or "deviant" based on their inability to eat certain foods. Children with food allergies are bullied and are often segregated from their peers during food-related events. While these books prepare children to disclose their needs to others, additional texts are necessary that address how to approach isolation and bullying by peers.

White Boys Everywhere and Their Mothers

I can easily summarize most of the picture books published in English that address food allergies as narratives about white boys with peanut allergies. These books are often self-published, and the authors, who usually self-identify as mothers, dedicate them to their sons who have food allergies. The stories usually follow the same arc: The readers are introduced to a young white boy with a food allergy; the child goes through an adjustment period during which they are upset that they can't eat peanuts or have to avoid certain foods; eventually they are accepted by their friends despite their allergy (or difference).

The stories gloss over the structural challenges of managing prescription drugs and copays, navigating complex school rules regarding food and medications, and dealing with bullying or isolation. For example, *Jude the Dude* is about a young white boy who is momentarily upset he cannot eat certain foods, but he quickly changes his mood and practices injecting epinephrine shots on his stuffed animals. The book imagines Jude's future: he grows up to be a football player, is elected mayor of his town, and has two children, including a little girl who is allergic to peanuts. In the sequel, Jude throws a "peanut-safe" Halloween party where all the friends he invites are white kids.[14] *My Food Allergies* was also written by a white mother who uses her son, Kieran, as a character. This text, like many others, includes advice to avoid sharing food, to ask adults to read labels to determine if the food contains allergens, to always carry injectable epinephrine, and to wear a bracelet that communicates your allergy and the necessity to seek medical attention in the event of an allergic reaction. *No Thank You, I'm Allergic: A Story about Food Allergy Awareness* tells the story of Jack, a young white boy with allergies to milk, eggs, and peanuts. It describes how Jack is encouraged to say, "No thank you, I'm allergic" when offered food from others. The straightforward medical advice offered in the book is the same as what is widely advised by medical authorities, especially around food avoidance and preparation.[15] Presumably the easiest way to remain "safe" is to avoid eating foods containing allergens and to carry a well-stocked medical kit, including injectable epinephrine, if needed, at all times. Tellingly, these texts usually don't discuss peer pressure or situations where the kid is isolated. (Sometimes, like Patty the pig, the child doesn't disclose their allergy, chooses to eat something they are allergic to, and has a reaction.)

Nor do these texts discuss the costs associated with remaining "safe." Presumably the authors have faced some challenges in parenting their child with food allergies, but these challenges don't make their way into the story. Rather these white children (mostly boys) are "protected" and encouraged to not let their allergy interrupt their childhood. I'm not necessarily faulting the parents and their desire to write these books, presumably as inspiration for their children, but I am struck by how many of them deal almost exclusively with young white boys who have peanut allergies, with few exceptions, and how the narratives are all so similar. These white authors reinforce the same storylines *again* and *again*. The risk of repeating these narratives is that the white allergic boy can be assumed to be *the* representative child, worthy of being kept innocent and protected. White boyhood becomes the marker of allergy despite epidemiological studies to the contrary. Although peanut is one of the most common allergens—one in the group of eight common allergens—milk and egg allergies are more common.[16] Yet these narratives show the seemingly innocent white boy with a food allergy struggling to understand why they have to avoid eating peanuts (and usually chocolate and baked goods because of the risk of cross-contamination). As I mention in the Introduction, white dominant narratives do not challenge the structural racism and white supremacy embedded in many allergy communities.

I was one of those young white boys with an allergy to peanuts, in addition to allergies to shellfish and tree nuts. I do not remember other kids with food allergies in grade school, but presumably they were my classmates (and maybe even friends). I suppose I also struggled at times to cope (or manage) my food allergy, but I do not find my own experience represented in these books. According to these texts, food allergy management, especially in the local public schools, appears to involve an expectation that your allergies will be anticipated by structures and programming already in place, including nut-free lunch tables and the availability of allergen-free snacks. These narratives also presume a heteronormative family unit with the means to be able to offer unlimited support with endless time and resources. There are no representations of having 504 plans or Individualized Education Plans approved to accommodate the child with food allergies in school, or of parents fighting to get their children's needs seen as valid. Much of the advocacy that is required is missing in these books. Instead, they remain testaments to white privilege, heteronormative family units, and financial resources to cover the expenses associated with the food allergy.

Princesses, Peanuts, and Cafés: Challenging the Individualization of Allergies

I opened this chapter by discussing *The Day I Met the Nuts*, which features a plot where an unnamed white boy creates a "NO NUTS ALLOWED!" club with other kids, most of whom have food allergies. This text gestures toward a communal response to food allergies where kids choose to forgo eating nuts to be together. *The Peanut-Free Café*, by another author, picks up on this theme but further destabilizes assumptions that food allergy is merely an individualized medical condition. Readers meet Simon, a white boy who eats only four foods: "bagels, green grapes, purple lollipops, and his favorite—peanut butter." Peanut butter is the "most popular food" at Simon's school, aptly named Nutley School. The conflict arises when Grant, a Black boy, shows up to school and announces he can't join the his fellow students and their peanut butter sandwiches at the lunch table: "Because if I eat one peanut or anything made with peanut oil, I can't breathe. I have to take my medicine right away." He lets the students know that at his last school "nobody ever ate peanut butter. Peanut butter was not allowed." This revelation shakes Simon; he had not realized that "his favorite food could make someone so sick," but he ultimately worries that his favorite food will no longer be allowed at school.[17] Even when the child with an allergy is not white, the text focuses on the white boy's desire and challenges in accommodating his friend. In an attempt to avoid a complete peanut ban, the principal, Ms. Filbert, sends home a note announcing a peanut-free table in the cafeteria open to any student with a peanut-free lunch.

Despite the announcement of the peanut-free space, during lunch Grant eats alone. Concerned the situation won't change, Principal Filbert consults various students (Simon, Zoe, a Black girl, and Jared, a disabled white boy) to ask for their advice.[18] The solution is a new flyer announcing a peanut-free café that features snacks, arts and crafts, and entertainment. A peanut-free lunch is all that is required to enter the café. The following day many white students and students of color bring peanut-free lunches to school to join Grant, except for Simon. Most of the kids at school swap out their peanut butter sandwiches for other foods, but Simon is unable to make the switch. Ostensibly a story about Grant and his peanut allergy, the book also highlights on a limited basis Simon's nutritional need to eat certain foods. Both boys need accommodation, yet the text presents Simon's inability to swap out peanut butter as the barrier to friendship and an ethics of accommodation. Ultimately it is Simon's needs that are not accommodated, making him the protagonist of the text. As readers, we do not get access to Grant's feelings or motivations. He is a plot device to extend the white boy narrative.

The following day, Simon's friends encourage him to eat pizza and join them at the café, but he eats alone. After another day of eating alone (and not enjoying his sandwich), Simon asks his mother to give him anything but peanut butter for lunch. His mom finds out that he can eat chili and prepares it for Simon's lunch. Again, readers aren't informed about Grant's desires or his understanding of the arrangement. We don't know, for example, if he preferred the peanut ban at his previous school over the willingness of his classmates to forgo eating peanut butter. Despite the diverse racial representation of the children in the school, the narrative centers the white boy and his needs over others.

This text does illustrate how most students are willing to forgo eating peanuts for the sake of the safety of their classmate. In fact, it appears that all students except Simon willingly trade their sandwiches for other lunches. Other than Grant with his food allergy, only one child, Jared, a white boy who uses a wheelchair, is a visibly disabled student at Nutley. Crip solidarity is displayed in the café by a white boy in a wheelchair. Yet Grant's limited role in the narrative shows how the multiracial text containing a Black child with an allergy turns into a white-dominant narrative about Simon with his unexplained nutritional needs and his success as the sign of making the community work.[19]

The solution here seems a bit tenuously tied to the willingness of the children to forgo peanut butter for the sake of their friend. There is no call for a complete ban of peanut products, which seems to have happened at Grant's previous school, as the café is supported only by the goodwill of Principal Filbert ("filbert" happens to be another name for a hazelnut). Here is where the challenge arises for the food-allergic child. At what point does asserting their need for peanut-free spaces become incompatible with the nutritional diversity of the others? I'm not merely talking about a desire to eat the occasional peanut butter sandwich, but rather a situation like Simon's, in which only a few foods are desirable or even are able to be eaten for whatever reason. I'm thinking of a young child my sister babysat that only ate chicken nuggets and tater tots for multiple years of his childhood. Presumably if another child were allergic to chicken, this boy would either not eat anything in the other child's presence, wait to eat the chicken later, or practice eating other things. One thing I really appreciate about *The Peanut-Free Café* is that Simon doesn't give up eating peanut butter altogether. Although his willingness and ability to eat chili seems sudden and unexpected, his dietary options are expanded because of his friendship with Grant and other students.

While the café might be temporary, and even the children's decision to refrain from eating peanuts must be made daily, there remains a type of performativity in the collective nut-free space. Like locations where individuals refuse to use scented products, these children are coming together to destabilize boundaries of bodily integrity. One child's allergy becomes the responsibility of the entire school to accommodate, and that set of circumstances is enabled by institutional resources. In a standard model of inclusion, policies and procedures often legislate admission or entry into a classroom or school. This model involves one unit telling another to accommodate a third party. Yet here there is no threat of legal enforcement or promise of a lawsuit to meet Grant's and Simon's differing needs.[20] Both children are accommodated—and presumably Grant is safe from the threat of an allergic reaction—yet the decision to participate in this mode of accommodation doesn't end with lawmakers or authority figures; rather, the children themselves enact an ethic of accommodation to ensure that Grant (and Simon) are included. (The other children, including Paul, Jared, and Zoe, encourage Simon to give up his sandwich to join the café. They don't want him left out of the fun, or to be isolated.) Eating is often a social activity, and the principal makes the café enticing by screening a movie there and offering safe snacks.

The Princess and the Peanut Allergy continues the theme of nonallergic children modifying their eating practices for the sake of their allergic friend. Regina and Paula, both young white girls, are best friends. Regina is planning a princess-themed birthday party, including serving a cake made with "rocky-road-nutty-fudge" brownies and "Peanut Butter Bunny Boogaloos" candy. Paula has a peanut allergy and is unable to eat any of the treats Regina is planning to serve at her party: "I can't eat your castle cake. I'm allergic to the bricks! And the towers will make me sick! I have a peanut allergy. I CAN'T EAT PEANUTS!" "Not even a peanut?" Regina wonders. Paula replies she can't: "Not even a teeny, tiny, small one. Once I ate one by mistake, and I had to go to the hospital! Now I always keep special medicine with me." Apparently their friendship up to this point did not involve cake or peanuts, because this revelation is surprising and upsetting to Regina. She asks Paula to pick the peanuts out of the treats, but understandably this is not a risk Paula is willing to take. The disclosure of the allergy and Paula's inability to eat the cake results in a shouting match between the best friends. Regina tells Paula she is "being a PAIN," and that "It's *my* party! *I'm* the princess here!" Paula replies, also claiming princess status, and each refuses to accommodate the other.[21]

"I wish Paula didn't have her peanut problem" Regina tells her mother, and she also quickly mentions her desire for the castle cake. Her mother encourages her to sleep on it and before bedtime encourages Regina to reread *The Princess and the Pea*. Of course, Regina realizes how the princess in the story felt the tiny pea under all the mattresses, and she makes the connection between peas and peanuts. Much like Simon, Regina is learning to realize how her food choices can hurt her friend. Regina changes her mind about the cake, prompting her to ask the baker to make a cake without any peanuts. She then calls Paula to apologize and let her know the cake will be peanut free. The book ends showing Paula and Regina next to a giant, pink princess-themed cake.

In a note at the end of the book, written by Scott Sicherer, MD, of the Jaffe Food Allergy Institute, there is a mention of "health and social challenges" that children with food allergies might face in situations like birthday parties and eating out. Indeed, both *The Princess and the Peanut Allergy* and *The Peanut-Free Café* highlight how the food-allergic child is at risk of being ostracized because others are unwilling to accommodate their disabilities. By refusing peanuts, the nonallergic kids can help the allergic kids to participate in the social and cultural rituals of their schools and friend circles. Yet both books are seemingly targeted toward the nonallergic, informing them of the risk present to others in their food choices. The princess party and the peanut-free café are created with the expectation that allergic children will be welcomed.

Another book with a similar title, *The Princess and the Peanut*, plays even more directly off the classic story *The Princess and the Pea*. It portrays the necessity of the nonallergic to forgo taking allergens to the castle. A maiden shows up at the castle late at night during a rainstorm. After the prince and his parents welcome the maiden to the castle, the queen asks the housekeeper to put a peanut (not a pea) under the visiting maiden's mattresses.[22] Almost immediately, the maiden has an anaphylactic reaction, prompting a visit from the palace doctor. Luckily the doctor has an injectable epinephrine shot with him that he promptly gives to the maiden. By undergoing allergy testing, she learns she is allergic to peanuts and tree nuts. The queen clears the castle of all foods that might contain peanuts or tree nuts, including the prince's favorite, peanut butter. Of course, the prince and maiden fall in love and live happily ever after, in a peanut-free and tree nut–free castle. Future allergic reactions are averted with a heavy dose of compulsory heterosexuality. The story again centers white men and their decisions to forgo eating nuts (or other allergens) for lovers, partners, children, parents, roommates, and the like. When the apartment, dorm room, cabin, house, or castle is declared to be nut free, the person with allergies does not have to worry that allergens will be brought into their living space. Accidents or mistakes happen, but the choice to live nut free (or dairy free, sesame free, alcohol free, etc.) for another person no longer means that the responsibility for remaining allergen free rests solely on the allergic individual but rather shifts to the community.

Even in the case of Grant, the narrative focuses on the dietary routine of Simon and the virtue of his ultimate willingness and ability to accommodate.

These narratives of communal acceptance and accommodation are narratives of whiteness and privilege. The allergic white boys (and occasionally white girls) and their supportive white parents (always heterosexual) assume that their needs will be understood as valid—and legitimate. The prince is the accommodating lover, reinforcing masculine protectionism and heteronormativity. There is no resistance or claims of being unreasonable. There are no calls for being homeschooled. When a need to be isolated from peanuts (or other allergens) is requested, other children choose to give up their allergen-filled foods to join their friends and classmates. But these expectations are not universal. In real life, children are denied schooling (which can also be a burden on their caregivers) because of severe disabilities, including allergies to peanuts and other substances. Assertions that the allergic child should be homeschooled are levied when accommodations are asked for. In addition, the messages of delayed consumption found in the books can be short lived, especially when systems of domination work by creating doubt about legitimacy or truth off the page. Only *some* peanut-allergic (white boys) are believed.

The ability to claim a life-threating allergy (and to be believed) is connected to whiteness, access to injectable epinephrine as a legitimizing device, gender and heterosexual normativity, economic resources (especially the resources to obtain a diagnosis), educational privilege to navigate bureaucracies that are unaccustomed to recognizing allergy protections under nondiscrimination law, and racial privilege wherein knowledge about one's body is immediately believed. Racial privilege also appears not only in material access but in narrative dominance, as illustrated by the analysis of several texts in this chapter. These narratives of food allergy reinforce white privilege, which continues to exclude food-allergic individuals of color and their families. On some level these children's books call for creating communities where individual needs are incorporated and treated as the needs of the whole. A few of them gesture toward such futures. Less prescriptive and less white-dominant narratives could challenge the liberal rights-bearing subject as the only one worth accommodating. A future where nutritional accommodations are welcomed (and anticipated) means that more of us can come to the table. At the table, we don't miss out on the chance to find folks to love, fight with, resist with, and make lasting connections with.

3

Allergic Reactions through Fluid Exchanges

But Jesus said to him, "Judas, are you betraying the Son of Man with a Kiss?"

LUKE 22:48 (NEW AMERICAN STANDARD BIBLE)

Standing before you, I ingest you. There is nothing fanciful about this. I am ingesting your exhaled air, your sloughed skin, and the skin of the tables, chairs, and carpet in this room.

MEL Y. CHEN, "TOXIC ANIMACIES, INANIMATE AFFECTIONS"

In a 2003 article entitled "The Kiss of Death: A Severe Allergic Reaction to a Shellfish Induced by a Good-Night Kiss," Dr. David Steensma of the Mayo Clinic reports on the case of a twenty-year-old woman's anaphylactic reaction that was triggered after she kissed her boyfriend. Roughly an hour prior to the kiss, the boyfriend had eaten shrimp, a known allergen for the young woman. Steensma cautions, "To my knowledge, this is the first report of a life-threatening reaction to shellfish transmitted by *passionate* kissing. Although most people are aware that passionate kissing can result in a variety of physical and emotional effects, patients with food allergies should be made aware that such intimate physical contact may present extreme dangers that are peculiar to their situation."[1]

In another article, titled "Kiss-Induced Allergy to Peanut: Food Allergy Transferred by Love," Swiss doctors Wüthrich, Däscher, and Borelli report on a case where a thirty-year-old man with severe peanut allergies that were diagnosed in childhood experienced an anaphylactic reaction after kissing his girlfriend. The authors write, "His girlfriend had eaten a few peanuts 2 h before and—knowing of the life-threatening reactions of her friend to hidden peanuts—she had brushed her teeth intensively, rinsed her mouth, and chewed chewing gum." Her preventive measures failed to remove all traces of protein residue. The amount of peanut protein necessary to provoke an allergic reaction can be quite small, as little as 50 µg (.05 mg), roughly one-fiftieth of a peanut. Accordingly, the authors conclude, "Kissing can constitute a severe danger for the food-allergic patient: therefore, before kissing, such patients should ask their lover what they have *just* eaten."[2]

Allergic reactions induced by kissing and other intimate interpersonal acts can present significant obstacles against spontaneous interactions for those with certain allergies. In both articles cited above, kissing that is deemed "passionate"—a seemingly subjective qualifier—marks an interaction as potentially precarious or even as deadly. More common portrayals of the "kiss of death" include the use of a kiss by a Mafia member to mark betrayal and impending execution, or biblical references to Judas Iscariot kissing Jesus Christ to identify him to Roman soldiers. When it comes to kissing while allergic, both case studies also offer statements of advice. When allergic individuals engage in acts of kissing, we are told, proper steps are needed to mitigate risk exposure. The clearest advice is to directly determine what has been consumed. Even though the second article inserts "just" before "eaten," it reports on a case where one individual ate peanuts two hours prior to the kiss and took various steps, including brushing of teeth, to eliminate any peanut residue. The shift from "2 hours prior" to "just" illuminates how assumptions about discreteness between time and presence of (allergen) residue blur. This leads us to wonder, At what point does peanut residue disappear? When is a kiss just a kiss? How are activities that can be expressions of love, desire, boredom, custom, duty, and so on interpreted when a thorough interrogation of potential allergens can precede such activities, particularly those that are generally very spontaneous? We might, for example, imagine an exchange between lovers: "Tell me about the pasta you had for lunch. Did it have a garnish? Are you sure the sauce was only tomato based? What about anchovies? Did it taste fishy?" Or between a couple in the early stages of dating: "Um, I think it was nut free. But I didn't really ask. I don't think I ate nuts today . . . did I?" A child to their mother: "Mom, did you remember to brush your teeth before coming over? I don't want your granddaughter to be covered in hives again after you kiss her." These hypothetical moments of dialogue sample the multiple ways in which, for allergic individuals and those in proximity, a kiss is never just a kiss.

In this chapter, I continue to trouble the assumption that food allergies demand isolated and individualized accommodations. In so doing, I challenge ideas about which types of accommodations are desirable or safe. For example, the act of kissing often involves the exchange of saliva between two people—if not also germs, food particles, and potential toxins. However, kissing is often construed, especially in sex education curricula, as a *safe* sexual practice, usually occurring between two people. Of course, kissing practices vary drastically from one person to another based on a variety of factors, including custom, age, and preference. Below, I also discuss situations where allergens are transmitted through semen, prompting anaphylactic reactions. Bodily fluids—namely saliva or semen—act as transmitters of allergens. In turning to such discussions, I attempt to destabilize discourses of risk, safety, community, and identity and argue that a critical disability studies approach to food allergies works to challenge assumptions that only those with class and racial privilege can demand safety and accommodation.[3] As elaborated below, asking a potential partner about their eating or grooming habits, or seeking medical treatment or allergy testing, depends on access to a variety of material and cultural resources. The allergic calculation is part of these conversations. Advocating for access or medical treatment and communicating needs—especially when connected to an impairment that might be assumed to be *made up*, or invisible, like food allergies—becomes easier for those with racial, gender, class, and ability privilege. Through a discussion of risks associated with kissing and intercourse—including allergies, HIV, other viruses, and bacteria—I also discuss consent and pleasure as key aspects in helping navigate intimacy to mitigate risk. I argue that communicating access needs enacts a type of interdependency, what Mia Mingus calls "access intimacy," a "kind of eerie comfort that your disabled self feels with someone on a purely access level."[4] Access intimacy affords opportunities to connect needs and desires by communicating intimate embodied knowledge.

Positionality

I begin by communicating portions of my embodied experiences and needs. I have a life-threatening allergy to tree nuts that requires me to carry injectable epinephrine. I grew up before the age of peanut bans in schools and widely available nut-free products. I became sexually active without thinking about risk of allergic reaction from fluid exchange. It was only later, when I had an allergic reaction because of cross-contamination at a restaurant, that I began to consider whether the choices I made were risky. I do remember becoming more diligent in communicating my allergies to restaurant servers and chefs, but not considering whether the people I was kissing or having sexual encounters with had eaten nuts. As a young, white, cisgender male, I was socialized to not think about my vulnerability. Indeed, my racial and gender privilege meant that it was expected that I take risks with a safety net while others experience heightened vulnerability. It was only much later, after studying critical disability studies and feminist and queer theory, that I was able to begin to articulate how experiences of safety and assumptions of risk were not evenly applied. At times I had allergic reactions even when I thought I was being safe. I came to learn about classmates and acquaintances who could not afford the copays and out-of-pocket expenses for injectable epinephrine or trips to the emergency room. When I was unemployed, without health insurance and using food stamps, I hoped my expired prescription would prevent an allergic reaction—and keep me out of the emergency room. Although I briefly mention my personal experiences of kissing and negotiating sexual partners, I simultaneously consider how disabled, queer, nonwhite, and otherwise marginalized individuals try to remain safe while navigating interpersonal moments when fluid is present. What are the queer, crip possibilities for pleasure as communicated through risk and need? In the following section, I discuss the relationship between kissing and risk, especially in relation to HIV and food allergies.

Kissing as an Exchange

In his text *The History of the Kiss!*, Marcel Danesi records various assumptions about the history of kissing as an expression of love and passion. One such assumption is that kissing might "be connected to the tendency of mothers to premasticate food for their offspring, that is, to chew their food and pass it on to their babies, mouth-to-mouth." Dansei continues,

> This makes some sense, since it posits that osculation [the act of kissing] derives from an action that ensured survival, encoded over-time into cultural practices and symbolism. But then how could an act born out of the love felt by a mother chewing food for her baby evolve into an act of pure romance? Supporters of the theory claim that a form of chewing between loves was once practiced in the Ziller Valley of central Europe. The exchange of premasticated substances between a male and a female was part of courtship. If a female accepted the wad, it meant she returned her partner's love.[5]

The connection between feeding a baby and the expression of love is tied to the passing of food from one to another via the mouth. While it seems reasonable for a parent to provide nutrition with prechewed food, perhaps doing so as part of the courting ritual (and expression of love) seems odd. Indeed, what might be the connection between sharing chewed food and commitment? Certainly, kissers of all types have passed gum while locking lips, but to share a bit of chewed brie and bread, or an Oreo or two, might seem counter to modern sensibilities. Yet the prechewing of food could help to accommodate a space-restricted esophageal tract or certain types of dental differences that cause chewing to be challenging—or various nutritional or eating practices that would benefit from partial transformation in texture, temperature, or color via mastication. The idea of receiving partially chewed food via a lover, parent, or friend also represents a type of interdependence in a moment of care—a use of the self (and the oral cavity) to benefit another. While kissing is mostly a courtship ritual, not delineating kissing as connected to courtship opens the possibility to consider additional possibilities (and risks) in locking lips. The act of kissing allows for the passing of fluid and matter.

Indeed, when two or more beings kiss, there is the potential for saliva, germs, allergens, or other matter to be exchanged. In thinking specifically about allergic reactions and bacteria and viruses, the discourse surrounding kisses, desire, and intimacy is illuminating in its delineation of which individuals can claim safety. In a chapter titled "There Are Such Things as Cooties," Sheril Kirshenbaum documents various "risks" associated with kissing. These include the passing of bacteria and viruses, including *Helicobacter pylori*, meningitis, and herpes simplex 1 (HSV-1). Of HSV-1, Kirshenbaum writes, "In truth, it's nearly impossible to avoid this virus as we go about our lives: An estimated 50 percent of us have acquired HSV-1 by the time we reach our teens, and 80 to 90 percent of the population tests positive by the age of fifty." While the "we" in the statement is unclear, perhaps referring to those residing in the United States, the seemingly nearly universal prevalence makes herpes a less-than-unique trait, although cold sores and genital herpes (which are associated with HSV-2) remain stigmatized markers. Kirshenbaum also reports on the ostensibly widespread prevalence of Epstein-Barr virus, which is known for causing mononucleosis, also referred to as the "kissing disease." After reporting on the prevalence of these risks, even if some are quite common, the text goes on to state that "one virus you probably do not need to be concerned about when it comes to kissing is HIV." Yet a few sentences later, Kirshenbaum reports that the Centers for Disease Control and Prevention (in the United States) "warns against 'prolonged-open mouth kissing' with someone known to carry HIV."[6]

Here we notice the discourses of certain viruses and bacteria as risky, even if those pathogens are seemingly universal. Other viruses (namely HIV) are deemed low risk but at the same time, in other contexts, remain closely asso-

ciated with discourses of fear, which are often intertwined with racist, homo-
phobic, and transphobic discourses. In addition, access to correct information
and reliable medication is heavily influenced by racial and class markers. Certainly one of the primary efforts of public health outreach, especially in the
United States around HIV and AIDS, was to address the fear of transmitting
HIV through "casual contact," including hugging and using public toilets, but
this effort is incomplete without also addressing heterosexism, racism, ableism,
and transphobia. Simply focusing on a discourse of safety without erasing
structural barriers to access and treatment maintains health disparities. Emily
Martin writes that during research for her book *Flexible Bodies*, wherein she
explores how understandings of immunity have shifted, including immunity
against HIV/AIDS, she still felt fear of transmission, even though she knew
casual contact was "safe."[7] Martin was fully aware of the factual data regarding
transmission but still felt fear because of the general AIDS-phobic culture she
lived in. Fear runs deep, especially in a society where certain populations are
constructed as contagious, dangerous, or risky to others.

On July 11, 1997, in the main section of the *Seattle Times*, appeared an article titled "Warning on Deep Kissing, HIV." The article read,

> Government scientists reiterated their warning that HIV-infected
> people should avoid deep kissing after a report that a man with
> bleeding gums apparently transmitted the virus to a woman through
> a kiss.
>
> It was the first reported case of HIV transmission through a kiss, but
> the Centers for Disease Control and Prevention emphasized that the
> virus was transmitted via the man's blood, not his saliva.
>
> There are no reported cases of people becoming infected with the
> AIDS virus through saliva.
>
> The CDC said the case is the very reason why, beginning in 1986,
> they started cautioning couples against deep kissing if one of them
> has the AIDS virus. Scientists are mostly concerned because of the
> possibility of bleeding gums—not saliva.
>
> "It's not likely, but we believe it can happen and that is the impor-
> tance of this case," said Dr. Scott Holmberg, a CDC epidemiologist.
>
> The man and woman had gum disease and poor oral hygiene. Her
> gum disease had weakened and thinned her gums, making it easier for
> the virus to get into her blood.
>
> Researchers have found a protein in saliva that keeps the virus from
> infecting white blood cells.

> Dr. Jerome Groopman, of the Beth Israel Deaconess Medical Center in Boston, said he encourages HIV-positive patients to restrict themselves to hugging and cheek-kissing.[8]

Imagine reading this article and encountering the following vague statements: "deep kissing," "It's not likely, but we believe it can happen," "protein in saliva," and "restrict themselves to hugging and cheek-kissing." Indeed, the article is full of contradictions: Individuals who are HIV positive are instructed to hug and only to kiss others on the cheek, while a protein in saliva is described as preventing transmission. Are individuals with *good* as opposed to *poor* dental hygiene *safe*? These is also no clarity about what constitutes "deep kissing." An AIDS-phobic populace must navigate a landscape where advice from medical professionals fails to provide clear directives. And perhaps most troubling, how are those closely affected by HIV/AIDS (through either diagnosis, relationships, partnership, vocation, or advocacy) expected to have full, spontaneous, and pleasurable lives and be active in their communities when discourses of actions are presented as risky? If you are recently diagnosed with HIV, do you stop kissing others? This example illustrates how an activity (such as kissing, which may or may not be deep) marks some as safe while others are at risk or dangerous. Individuals are sometimes making decisions based on incomplete or contradictory information.

Because of inadequate access to medical resources and varying degrees of autonomy over individual bodies, ideas about which practices are ultimately safe from a public health perspective might not address how individuals negotiate discourses of risk, spontaneity, and desire. I cannot recall ever asking someone I was kissing (or about to kiss) about their dental and oral hygiene, or if they were HIV positive. Yet I have (sometimes) paid attention to (and inquired) whether my kissing buddy had eaten nuts. Why did I assume kissing presented little risk for HIV transmission but not allergic reaction? Or how does one activity become safe while another is risky? Quite simply, to take food allergies as an example, individuals might prefer to kiss their date while negotiating the risk that allergens are present. Or being in the "heat of the moment" might mean that questions about food allergens are not always high priority. Or, taking my life as an example, I grew up occasionally kissing others, not realizing I should have been asking if they had recently eaten nuts. Was I risking a reaction by locking lips? If I had asked, would the kiss not have occurred? Is kissing more enjoyable *with* risk? Does communicating one's needs allow for letting go enough to enjoy the presence and body of another? Of course, being safe is not always desired. The allergic calculation might determine if I/others/we are kissing.

Indeed, there is a certain amount of class-, racial-, ability-, and gender-based privilege embedded in discourses of safety, especially when safety stands in for being unable to depend on the actions or information supplied by another. Individuals take risks daily for a variety of reasons, from bicycling without a helmet to skipping a dose of medication. Choosing safety might not be the most attractive, or frankly an available, option. In discussing mantras of "safe sex" and the practice of barebacking, Tim Dean argues, "These days virtually everyone imagines that the safe-sex maxim 'Use a condom every time' does not apply to him or her but to those whose pleasure seems less significant or legitimate than his or her own. Fucking without a condom is often regarded as a privilege of the normatively coupled in the age of AIDS."[9] Below, I discuss allergic reactions and sexual intercourse, but I find Dean's theorization helpful for contextualizing all acts of fluid exchange. Which acts are *safe*, from a public health perspective? Which actions are *desirable*? Is safety desirable? Of course, even if oral sex, for example, is construed as an activity during which an individual can encounter a sexually transmitted infection, oral sex for some people may still be the most frequently practiced sexual activity, or the most preferred. Or even the safest type.

In the chapter in her book on "cooties," Kirshenbaum lists the riskiest "kisses," including vampire biting (framed as a type of "immortal" kiss); kissing a dead bat (a type of necrophilic interspecies kiss); or an allergic reaction induced by a kiss (an allergic kiss). It is telling that Kirshenbaum places allergic reactions via kissing alongside less socially acceptable types of kissing to position the food allergic as abnormal. Kirshenbaum writes, "You might think you're out with the perfect person, about to embark on an epic romance. All the signals seem right, and you go in for the kiss. But suddenly, instead of being excited and aroused, you—or your partner—is covered with hives."[10] Hives, a sign of an allergic reaction, mark the kiss as dangerous. Due to perceived, actual, or experienced risk, food-allergic individuals might avoid dating or other activities in which negotiating risks of reactions or expectations of kissing might possibly occur.

Communicating Risk of Reaction

In an April 2014 edition of *Allergic Living* magazine's column "Ask the Experts," a teenager with food allergies asks about the safety of kissing. The expert, Dr. Hemant Sharma, writes that in two studies, "between 5 and 12 percent of patients surveyed" reported an allergic reaction after kissing. Sharma also reports on an additional study in which peanut allergens were present in saliva four hours after eating peanuts. In *The Ultimate Guidebook for Teens with Food*

Allergies, Tess Bantock writes, "When I was dating my high school boyfriend, we definitely had more than a few mix-ups with my allergies. One evening, when we were watching a movie, he kissed me after eating one of my allergens in a snack that he prepared and ate in another room. After a few minutes, my face became extremely itchy and I ran to the bathroom to discover that I was covered in hives. As the symptoms progressed, I made the decision to use my auto-injector and was taken to the hospital."[11]

For Bantock, a romantic moment turned potentially deadly when she kissed her boyfriend. Risk of reaction exists when interacting with the lips of another. One way to negotiate risk, desire, and kissing is to communicate with prospective partners about issues related to food allergy and transmission. Sloan Miller devotes an entire chapter in her book *Allergic Girl: Adventures in Living Well with Food Allergies* to negotiating dating (and kissing). Miller advocates that food-allergic individuals have what she calls the "food-allergy talk": "This is not a where-is-the-relationship-going talk. Not at all. This is an I-need-to-tell-you-something-about-me-so-we-can-have-the-best-time-ever talk. It's purely informational. It's a medical fact about you. Remember, connect to your food-allergy needs without shame, embarrassment, or apology; communicate those needs clearly, assertively, and graciously; and recognize you have options."[12]

Miller gives textual examples of the food-allergy talk, ranging from the humorous (with a reference to Vince, played by John Travolta, stabbing Mia, played by Uma Thurman, in the heart with adrenaline in *Pulp Fiction*) to the more direct: "I have food allergies. If you want to kiss me as much as I want to kiss you, please don't eat any tree nuts or salmon. I'm really allergic to those and can't kiss you if you eat them." In the direct version, Miller uses desire as the motivator to communicate needs. Practically, this version allows for spontaneity in the future through communicating about issues of accommodation in the present. Recognizing the potential for exchange of saliva and allergens, the food allergy talk might help mitigate any lasting concerns regarding transmissibility of allergens via romantic courting rituals. Miller, however, cautions that prospective partners, or one-time kissing buddies, much like family members, coworkers, and friends, might need continual reminders of how to negotiate personal contact while remaining "safe." She highlights that these needs should be communicated without shame. As have many who attempt to advocate for accommodations, Miller has been ridiculed for asserting her needs: "I forged ahead, taking out the autoinjector of epinephrine just so he could see it, but Adam wasn't listening. He seemed very focused on making loud, inappropriate jokes—about me, about food allergies, and about Benadryl. Even the diners at the next table looked over with sympathetic glances. It was obvious: this date was tumbling downhill, and fast. We had spent the earlier part of the evening trying to find common ground, without succeeding, and now this."[13] Miller's willingness to share this experience with her readers illustrates how communicating information about your dependence on another is not without risk of rejection. Yet Miller's position as a light-skinned, educated, respected member of the United States food allergy advocacy community hints at how one's ability to be knowledgeable about one's body—and to communicate that knowledge to others—is a privilege that is too often unevenly distributed along the lines of class, gender, race, ability, and educational status.

Even if access needs are communicated, however, the interaction between time (e.g., the moment of consumption, the time of the encounter, the last effort to eliminate allergens, the time of day) and matter (e.g., food residue and fluids such as saliva) might not be as neatly delineated. It can be challenging to determine how these two seemingly disparate things are connected. More explicitly, even though time can be measured by the passing of minutes and hours, how can one issue (the desire to avoid consuming transmitted allergens, which can be measured and felt) be connected to another (waiting a certain amount of time for allergens to disappear)? On a date in which allergens are consumed, how can those involved in the potential kiss (or other exchange) be sure that the allergens disappear, especially if given the advice to wait? Miller recounts a date in which her partner consumed shellfish, an allergen for Miller, prior to their meeting. Miller suggested the two consume a safe meal of burgers before kissing: "We need to wait a bit and eat a nonallergenic meal." Miller continues, "Midway through our allergy-safe dinner, he smiled and said, 'May I kiss you now?' We had a big smooch-a-thon right there at the burger restaurant. Fishy crisis averted, and we had a great date."[14] Prioritizing consent, this interaction is modeled as one that maintains the balance between safety and sexiness. Still, although she does not mention it, Miller kissed her date with the risk that fish or another allergen would be transmitted via saliva.

Miller recounts another example of a client of hers, Ben, who was on a date at a dance club. His date, Paul, ate a chocolate that contained hazelnuts, thus jeopardizing Ben's safety (and ability to kiss Paul). After explaining to Paul that the chocolate contained hazelnuts, and that food ingredient labels might not address issues of cross-contamination, Ben recalls,

> You [Sloane] had sent me the peanut study that demonstrates that the only thing to do is wait and eat something else. "Here, eat this apple." I quickly thrust the safe snack I had with me into his hand. Paul happily obliged. While he was eating, I described the study so Paul could have

some background. Paul listened, eyes widening. "Okay, so let's wait a
few hours to be safe," Paul said. I reached around to grab his hand, but
he stopped me. "Just to be safe, let me wash my hands before you do
that. I wouldn't want to hurt you."[15]

Referring to clinical studies about the potential for peanut residue to remain,
both Miller and Ben communicate to their dates the necessity of taking certain actions to increase the potential for safe (and perhaps more passionate)
kissing. Despite also trusting in the passing of time to ensure that they prevent
an allergic reaction, both individuals act while knowing a risk remains for a
reaction. Spaces between teeth and gums can hold particles of almonds, and
dental appliances can trap cheese residue. These kisses, although most likely
benign, still carry risk. The interactions also place consent as central. Miller's
date directly asks, "May I kiss you now?" Feminist efforts to address sexual and
interpersonal violence have highlighted the necessity of expanding understandings and practices of consent.[16] They have also highlighted the fact that
the ability to consent is often denied because of racist, classist, or ableist ideas
about which bodies are "pure," "innocent," or able to experience violence.

While recognizing that consent as a construct has the potential to uphold
rationality and agency that might reinforce racist, ableist, patriarchal systems
of power, I find the examples of Miller and Ben helpful in thinking about how
food-allergic individuals can communicate about and actively negotiate their
needs with their lovers, dates, or strangers, who may have competing or com-
plementary needs. The idea of describing a medical condition to a potential
partner, especially after an initial meeting, can be daunting. As most first dates
involve sharing a meal, moments of potential allergen consumption are plentiful, especially when individuals have multiple allergies. Having clear strategies for effectively communicating the potential for an allergic reaction can
assist in facilitating accommodating relationships that are based on reciprocity. In addition, the process of communicating interdependence ("please don't
eat nuts") shifts the burden of safety and embodiment from an individual to a
shared action of reciprocity. In turn, the accommodation becomes enacted
through a communicated commitment to destabilizing discourses of safety,
risk, and community beyond an individualized approach. A. J. Withers writes
of "radical access" as that which acknowledges "systemic barriers that exclude
people, particularly certain kinds of people with certain kinds of minds and/
or bodies, and work[s] to ensure not only the presence of those who have been
left out, but also their comfort, participation and leadership. Spaces that need
to incorporate radical access principals are organizational, they are educational

and institutional, but they are also the spaces closest to us: our cafés, our offices, our homes and our hearts." Withers importantly highlights that access "doesn't just begin at the front door" but involves transformation to address systemic and interpersonal rejection.[17]

Yet despite the best attempts to track the presence of allergens (or viral loads), certainty is not ensured, and individuals act with varying levels of risk. Mia Mingus writes that "access intimacy is something I am coming to understand that I need in my life; something that I cannot (and don't want to) live without. I need it to literally be my whole self because access is such an intimate part of my life as a queer physically disabled woman of color adoptee. Without it, relationships exist under a glass ceiling or split by thick frosted windows, with huge pieces of myself never being able to be reached. Without it, there is survival, but rarely true, whole connection." Both Mingus and Withers are articulating how their experiences of oppression inform their desire to create radical moments of connection. This connection is related to embodiment. By communicating needs, or bodily difference, an assemblage shifts access from the individual to the whole. Mingus refers to access intimacy as "interdependence in action." Mingus importantly acknowledges that this interdependence means "someone else is with me in this mess." Accordingly, "The power of access intimacy is that it reorients our approach from one where disabled people are expected to squeeze into able bodied people's world, and instead *calls upon able bodied people to inhabit our world.*"[18] For someone with multiple food allergies or chemical sensitivities, for example, the world can be downright hostile and violent. Inaccessible options for safe foods, chemical-laden bathrooms, hidden allergens, or traces of toxic cologne limit an individual's ability to navigate spaces and be present and spontaneous. Communing with others is challenging or impossible without a risk to oneself. Yet being open to radical access and intimacy—indeed, interdependence—creates a deeper connection that shifts the traditional way inclusion is understood. For example, if a friend or lover refuses to consume, buy, or serve nuts, that action of refusal transforms our relationship and shifts my access needs, changing them into the needs of the community. As the space becomes nut free, I can relax and create meaningful connections based on my entire self.

Mingus calls this "shared work," a recognition that those without disabilities are active participants in solidarity. Mingus writes that access intimacy is an "antidote to the pain and the extreme isolation that pound like crashing waves with no end. It has been a way to remember my magnificence and my dignity. It has been the tender balm and recognition of parts of me that most people would rather deny, avoid and pretend away."[19] When another person incorporates my access needs, they are making a choice to change their ontology to align with mine. Traditional discourses of inclusion center on one entity deciding that another can gain access—for example, a court ruling that a child with a service animal should be allowed to be educated with her peers. One entity with more power (the court) instructs the school district (with less power) to *allow* a child (with almost no structural power) to attend class. Unlike inclusion, access intimacy is a means of shifting our relations: "transforming what counts as valuable and reinforcing the ways we depend upon each other." Susan Wendell, in *The Rejected Body*, writes about the value of interdependence: "if everyone with a disability is to be integrated fully into my society, without being 'the Other' who symbolizes moral failure, then social ideals must change in the direction of acknowledging the realities of our interdependence and the value of depending on others and being depended upon."[20]

In the next section, I continue exploring the value and necessity of interdependency, while discussing allergic reactions via sexual fluid exchange. Discourses of safe sex and infection try to delineate certain practices and populations as low risk. How can risk be acknowledged while also encouraging pleasure and desire?

What about Sex?

The discourse around sexual activity, especially in classrooms in the United States, is that sex is risky. Different sexual activities also seem to carry different levels of risk. Even assumptions about risk are not applied equally. Normatively coupled, white, heterosexual, suburban teenagers may be told that sex is risky because it might result in pregnancy and an interruption in their ability to progress onto higher education. Assumptions about higher education as a natural progression for certain (white) children certainly influences statements that intercourse will lead to pregnancy. Other sexual activities (and those bodies that might practice such activities) are also construed as risky. As mentioned above, there remain a tremendous number of AIDS-phobic responses to types of sexual activity, for example, anal sex between men. In addition, bodies become symbols in heteronormative, ableist, white supremacist settings, for example, linking gender identity or racial status to infection prevalence without addressing the structural inequalities that maintain the inequalities. As Abby Wilkerson remarks, "Cultural erotophobia is not merely a general taboo against open discussions of sexuality, and displays of sexual behavior, but a very effective means of creating and maintaining social hierarchies, not only those of sexuality, but those of gender, race, class, age, and physical and mental ability."[21] Individuals negotiate levels of risk daily (in modes of transportation or culinary choices or recreational activities), but when it comes to sexual activity, assumptions of risk are not universally applied. For example, white heterosexual undergraduates "hook up" with some regularity, yet individuals with intellectual disabilities, even college students with intellectual disabilities, can be discouraged from sexual activity—or even prohibited because of competency laws or similar regulations. My point here is that linking risk to actions can reproduce inequalities that seem to make these risks appear "real," as opposed to historically and culturally produced discourses that additionally have material impacts on bodies. Someone else's risk is "real" and should be managed, while an individual might consider their risk level manageable, negligible, nonexistent, or even desirable. Labeling another's practices or choices as risky carries differential levels of power and privilege.

In thinking specifically about sexual activity, a variety of activities can involve the exchange of bodily fluids. Almost exclusively these fluids (especially blood and semen) are considered to potentially carry infections (such as gonorrhea) but not to transmit allergens. There are multiple questions involving assumptions of risk, sexual activity, bodily fluids, and allergens: If saliva can transmit allergens, can other bodily fluids, including semen and vaginal secretions, also transmit allergens? Is there a different risk of transmission for allergic individuals? Are allergic reactions possible from exposure to allergens delivered through fluids present because of sexual activity? Documented allergic reactions via kissing are well known, but allergic reactions triggered via sexual activity are less familiar to the public. Certainly, sexual activity is connected to fluid exchange, in terms of either limiting exchange via barrier methods (dental dams, condoms) or facilitating exchange (by not using condoms). The fact that condomless sex is referred to as "unprotected sex" illustrates how sexual activity—and more explicitly the exchange of body fluid during sexual activity—is construed to pose a threat to childless or infection-free futures.

The *Daily Mail*, a tabloid newspaper, reported in 2011 on a woman who experienced an allergic reaction shortly after having sexual intercourse with her boyfriend. The woman's boyfriend ate a handful of Brazil nuts prior to initiating their sexual activities. The boyfriend brushed his teeth, rinsed his mouth, and thoroughly cleaned his hands and fingernails, steps the paper refers to as "extreme precautions." After the two had sex, the woman had trouble breathing, and her lower body began to swell. When she sought medical treatment, doctors initially assumed the allergens had been transmitted via saliva and sweat, but after the couple disclosed the precautions they had taken it was determined that the Brazil nut protein was transmitted via the boyfriend's semen. The article continues:

> It is the first recorded case of an allergic reaction to Brazil nuts through intercourse.
>
> To be absolutely certain, doctors brought the man back in and took two semen samples—one before, and one four hours after eating Brazil nuts.
>
> They then performed a test on the girl, where they give a small injection with a needle covered in semen underneath the skin.
>
> This is a common way to test for particular allergies.
>
> It appears that Brazil nut proteins resist digestion, which is why they generally end up in the immune system, triggering immune reactions.
>
> They discovered the woman's skin swelled up and his semen caused a reaction just three to four hours after eating the nuts.
>
> But because the couple split up after the reaction, scientists were not able to carry out further tests.[22]

The clinical article about the case, published four years prior to the newspaper article, includes a photograph of the skin-prick test results that confirmed the reaction to semen containing Brazil nut protein.[23] The image portrays a wheal (red bump) on the woman's skin. I was struck by the inclusion of the image, but not because it is out of the ordinary. Completing a skin prick test is standard protocol and is often the first type of allergy test that will occur in a physician's office. One of the benefits of the test is that it is easily administered and does not require significant time to process. As someone interested in examining the cultural implications of food allergies, I was struck by the reproduction of the image as evidence of nut proteins in semen. Access to technology that can isolate a protein is limited to locations such as labs. In this case, readers notice evidence of a reaction captured at a particular moment. The moment of reaction was temporal, and with each passing minute the allergic reaction either becomes more severe or decreases in intensity. Readers are not shown the semen as the fluid of transportation but are nevertheless forced to think of semen (and any associations they might have with the substance) in the discussion of the case.

In addition, it is unclear why the *Daily Mail* reported on this case four years after it was published in a peer-reviewed scientific journal. It seems that a blog, *io9*, affiliated with *Gawker* posted the story before the *Daily Mail*.[24] In both articles the allergic reaction is used to shock or create humor. The skin prick testing with semen seems to provoke ridicule and is offered up as self-evidently ridiculous, despite the skin prick test being a standard method of allergy testing. It appears that the use of sperm is what seems odd, despite it being essential to the inquiry if the fluid contained allergens. The story, perhaps predictably, was regrettably reposted and blogged about with the addition of multiple sexist jokes.

A more recent occurrence of an allergic reaction triggered via sexual encounter involved two teenage males. According to the clinical article, a male with a history of peanut allergy and asthma received oral sex from another male who had recently eaten peanut butter, unknown to the allergic male. Ultimately the one with a history of food allergies died because of an anaphylactic reaction. The authors comment that this was the first case of a man having sex with a man that resulted in an allergic reaction, and they speculate that the allergen was transmitted via oral mucosa. (The two men did not kiss.)[25]

The authors of the clinical article about the allergic reaction involving the Brazil nut write that they ruled out an allergy to semen. Allergy to human seminal fluid is well documented in women. In a 2004 article, Shah and Panjabi reviewed the eighty documented cases published in English of women being allergic to seminal fluid, referred to as human seminal plasma allergy. Recommendations for managing the allergic reaction include consistent condom usage as a barrier method to prevent the introduction of semen from one partner to another—unless one of the partners has an allergy to latex, in which case condoms made of other materials can be used. An exception is also discussed for those with a desire to reproduce. To manage risk, those with allergic reactions are asked to participate in sexual activities that prevent the sharing of fluids. Discourses of risk and linkages to safe sex reemerge. Shah and Panjabi also report on three cases where an individual experienced an allergic reaction through exposure to antigens present in semen, including vinblastine, dicloxacillin, and walnut protein.[26]

Brazil nut proteins are described as resisting digestion. Marcos Alcocer, Louise Rundqvist, and Göran Larsson report on one of the proteins in Brazil nuts: Ber e 1, described as the "major allergen" of the nut. In the 1990s, efforts to biotechnologically enhance crops included the transferring of Brazil nut protein into tobacco, beans, canola, and potato, among other crops. Yet despite these crops achieving increased levels of protein, the allergenicity of the crops (because of Ber e 1) prevented commercial applications. In these bioengineered crops, the protein structure of the Brazil nut maintains its identity as a source of allergen. In a *New York Times* article that discusses how genetically engineered crops can cause allergic reactions, Dr. Rebecca Goldberg, senior scientist for the Environmental Defense Fund, a nonprofit environmental advocacy group, notes, "Since genetic engineers mix genes from a wide array of species, other genetically engineered foods may cause similar health problems. People who are allergic to one type of food may suddenly find they are allergic to many more." The newspaper article samples perspectives of various scientists and concludes that more regulations are needed to ensure genetically modified products carry appropriate labels and are tested for the presence of allergenic proteins. One of the many theories about the rise in food allergies in places like the United States and Canada links it to the rise of consumable genetically modified crops. The reason that allergic reactions seem to be increasing remains under dispute, but what becomes clear is that certain proteins, here Ber e 1, resist modification (or digestion) and infiltrate semen or soybeans. The allergenic substances in fluid are *animated* in their ability to provoke a reaction. I am reminded of Mel Y. Chen's theorization of toxic animacies and the "potential queer exchange" I discuss in Chapter 1. In the above example, that the semen contained the allergen only three to four hours after the person ate the Brazil nuts highlights how quickly the protein infiltrates bodily fluid. As Bansal et al. argue, "To enter the semen the protein would require circulation in the blood to the prostate or other reproductive organs."[27] The semen becomes allergenic. In trying to understand the process, the clinicians obtained samples of semen to trace the amount of protein and how quickly the protein became an active allergen in the fluid.

While Brazil nuts are not a chemical, tracking chemical levels in bodily fluids is a public health strategy to track exposure entangled in what Monica Casper and Lisa Jean Moore call "biomonitoring":" Biomonitoring is an extractive technology; that is, liquids and tissues must be removed from human bodies in order to be manipulated and assessed. Thus, it is not whole bodies that are measured but leaky and diaphanous bits and parts, such as breast milk and blood; these stand in for and are made to represent whole persons—indeed, entire communities and the species writ large." One of the goals of biomonitoring includes determining "individual and species risk," as bodies can become "toxic waste dumps." Since the 1970s, individual exposure to chemicals, including lead, has been measured through examination of various bodily fluids. The measured level of chemicals in the body at a given time is known as the "body burden." The term "burden" here connects to heavy loads, or a feeling of being weighed down. Lead or bisphenol-A, for example, can affect thyroid or kidney function. Casper and Moore discuss how breast milk is monitored to determine exposure to chemicals, yet monitoring of the individual frequently stands in for monitoring entire populations. Sperm, however, linked to individual bodies, is "strong and tenacious" and a "sneaky and leaky silent witness." They conclude, "The process of extracting material from human bodies, while framed as useful for the social body writ large, is not done democratically," and "a core idea of biosurveillance is that knowledge may enable risks to be minimized . . . but risks for and to whom, and from what?"[28]

Semen as a fluid is assumed to carry risk of fertilization (pregnancy) or infection (STIs), or to be part of an act of aggression (sexual assault), but not often to trigger an allergic reaction. Brazil nuts can contain higher levels of radium compared with other foods, and due to the high level of selenium per nut, eating more than six to eight nuts a day has the potential to lead to toxicity. Eating Brazil nuts carries (some) risk, yet this risk is not evenly distributed because not all consumers are allergic, or would encounter semen, and not all nuts have high(er) levels of radium.[29] Using dental dams, condoms, or similar barrier methods can offer a level of protection from fluids that contain allergens, especially if sexual partners are unsure of consumption. Many of the suggestions above regarding the impact of sharing embodied knowledge can be applied with sexual partners. While it seems that the risk of allergic reaction via sexual activity is lower than via kissing, allergic individuals can communicate risk to partners to shift negotiation to all involved.

Allergenic Fluid: What Is a Person Supposed to Do?

In this chapter, I have discussed ways in which practicing interdependency allows individuals to be intimate while allergic. This type of relationship between oneself and others balances risk with desire and pleasure. This section heading asks, "What is a person supposed to do?" For many, the answer is straightforward. Avoid situations (and activities) where fluids might contain allergens. Not kissing others when they have consumed a known allergen and avoiding sexual contact provides the clearest way to remain safe. Yet this solution can be lacking because it proscribes a pattern of action that demands conformity—and the complete cooperation of others. Certainly, partners can practice eating that avoids encountering allergens, and many folks regularly participate in sexual activity that contains fluids. However, both types of practices depend on trusting the other partner to not eat the allergen. Failing to trust, or wanting additional measures for protection, might also require an individual to carry multiple injectable epinephrine shots and antihistamine pills, have medical insurance, and know where the nearest emergency room is located.

In *Curative Violence*, Eunjung Kim asks, "What would disability studies approaches to infectious diseases and public health look like?" Kim challenges a narrow approach to human rights that depends on discourses of curability and lack of contagion. While Kim's focus is on Hansen's disease, and specifically antistigma campaigns in Korea, she traces out additional discussions of infection from disability studies scholars, including work by Catherine Kudlick (smallpox) and Christopher Bell (HIV). Of Bell's work, Kim writes, "Bell's provocative initiation of a queer disability studies approach to infectious disease from the point of pleasure and desire of infected persons should inform how to empower ethical readings of cultural images of infectious diseases from the perspectives of lived experiences and social relations." Bell writes of efforts to exchange money for sexual encounters with men in locations throughout the globe. In these exchanges, Bell negotiates spontaneity, his pleasure (and that of his partners), in an AIDS-phobic culture that expects him to disclose his HIV-positive status. Failure to "disclose" is often criminalized, and Bell cites cases where individuals were convicted for not telling individuals about their serostatus.[30]

In teaching Bell's article, I often face student responses that want to criticize Bell's choices, especially for putting his partners at risk. Risk here is assumed to lead to infection. Of course, when people have sex for a variety of reasons, there might be varied levels of communication about past partners, practices, or even presence of infectious diseases. Additionally, oral sex might be considered "not sex" or a safe alternative to vaginal or anal intercourse. That Bell is largely performing oral sex on the individuals he gives money to does not seem to assuage the concern of (some) students. I ask why, and often receive the immediate reaction that because he is positive, he should disclose. In this framework, the responsibility supposedly rests with the individual. Bell writes,

> I was twenty-three years old when I was diagnosed as HIV-positive; I
> am now thirty-four. Previously, I never would have imagined that I
> would pay individuals for sex or that I would do so while not, in some
> instances, disclosing my status. I'm not the man I used to be. Admittedly, I may not be "responsible" as determined by conventional
> norms, but that doesn't immediately relegate me to the realm of
> "irresponsibility." Some of my behaviors might dwell in that realm, but
> I don't have to be positioned there, or position myself there, in totality
> or permanently. I can occupy a middle space, moving toward and away
> from responsibility and irresponsibility as circumstance, agency, and
> desire dictate.[31]

To answer Kim's question, I agree it is instructive to revisit Bell's negotiation between a middle space of desire and pleasure framed by circumstances and discourses of risk. Whose risks are named as such? And which actions, even if risky, are assumed to be standard practices of dating, or hooking up, or just being a white nondisabled heterosexual? In discussing sexually transmitted infections, certain populations are construed as "at risk" or as "super predators." To be certain, these labeled groups are populated with people from oppressed positions. Often, labeling a practice as risky, or a person at risk, can hide the forces that constrain access to information or resources, what is referred to as "structural violence."[32] One difference between these discourses of "at risk" populations and people with food allergies is that management for those with allergies is based on personal choices, or discourses of responsibility. For example, I might think that it is my responsibility to ensure I carry my prescription drugs, or know what foods are safe for me to eat, or if my partner has consumed nuts. Action depends on the individual, even if I should act based on incomplete information from another. Here is where the limits of this approach fail to address how to negotiate passion, spontaneity, risk, and contagion. If, as a food-allergic person, I want to eat, or kiss, or have sex with another, how do I act in real time? What steps are necessary for the preparation of acting with intent while maintaining robust discourses of pleasure and safety, if desired? The above example from Sloane Miller of the necessity to communicate needs is a helpful place to start. I wonder, what is missing in this approach? How can this conversation be queered/cripped to expose what assumptions are embedded?

In this chapter, I have sketched out examples of reactions through fluid exchange. While small (and potentially fatal) in number, these examples allow for individuals to get a sense of the types of negotiations food-allergic individuals make, especially connected to sexual contact. In presenting these cases, I have tried not to sensationalize them but rather to think through the way risk, agency, and choice are presented, while also trying to center a discourse of pleasure. In tracing out linkages between people with Hansen's disease, HIV, and food allergies, what types of contagion (and/or transmission) connect groups of people rarely (if ever) in coalition?

Mia Mingus writes, "In my life access intimacy continues to be a game-changer, a way to queer access into a tool we can use to get free. It has been a way to shift and queer how I and others understand disability and ableism." Mingus continues, "And because of the inherent interdependence of access intimacy—the 'we' of access intimacy—it has transformed the kinds of conversations I am able to have with some of the able bodied people in my life."[33] In practicing interdependence, access intimacy negates the medicalization of disability. Imagine two lovers at a restaurant informing the waiter of a food allergy, yet only one of the diners has a diagnosed allergy. The motivation of the two is to enjoy a meal out without concern of consuming allergens and impeding a night of lovemaking. That only one of the two has an allergy does not matter to the medical industrial complex, but for that moment one incorporates the allergy of another to facilitate spontaneity and desire. This is a type of access intimacy.

While kisses might still be precarious because of cross-contamination or forgotten bites, allergic individuals can navigate interpersonal moments of desire and spontaneity. Practicing interdependency shifts expectations of individualized accommodations toward a relational effort. Radical crip queer space recognizes risk while also acknowledging passion and spontaneity.

4
You Ate What?

Intentionality, Accidents, and Death

During episode twelve of the Korean television drama *Romance Is a Bonus Book* (2019, 로맨스는 별책부록), Song Hae-rin (Jung Yoo-jin) drinks two kettles of cucumber soju.[1] What would be an unremarkable drink choice for many is the opposite for Hae-rin, as she is allergic to cucumbers. As part of the love-square plot line, Hae-rin purposely chooses to make and drink the cucumber-laced soju. After Hae-rin passes out at a bar, Ji Seo-joon (Wi Ha-joon) calls Cha Eun-ho (Lee Jong-suk) to come take Hae-rin home. Seo-joon tells Eun-ho that Hae-rin made the soju to "feel better." The next morning, Hae-rin is greeted by her coworkers at Gyeoroo Publishing Company, who notice the red hive marks on her face and ask with exasperation, "Did you eat cucumbers again?" "If you had known that, you should have been more careful. Can't you tell by the smell? Cucumbers have a peculiar smell." She replies, "I ate them on purpose. I was hurting so much, so I just wanted to die." One of her coworkers, Bong Ji-hong (Jo Han-chul) remarks, "But you don't die. You get better pretty quickly."

Indeed, Hae-rin has not died, *yet*, from eating cucumbers, but she does eat them to feel better—by feeling ill. The allergen (here cucumbers) creates a reaction that helps bring forth a desired feeling. Despite the mixture of exasperation, blame, and dismissal from others, she eats the allergen, remembering her previous level of reaction and hoping for a similar one this time. She takes the risk that the reaction will not be more severe than her last one. This fictional example illustrates how Hae-rin inflicts self-pain during emotional distress, portraying one type of motivation some allergic individuals use when deciding how to negotiate eating (or drinking). The mantra of avoidance as the way to manage allergen consumption does not work for all. As Dayna Glabau argues, "purity easily translates from necessary practices to exclusionary principles, from protecting an individual's body in ways appropriate for them to limiting exposure to all kinds of people who might be carrying or cooking with the food that might pose a threat."[2] Once again, discourses of purity and safety interact with those of risk and accident when individuals might be just a bite away from a life-threatening allergic reaction. In this chapter, I explore the various motivations people follow in eating allergens, sometimes even intentionally. Accidents happen, of course, but rarely are stories about why people choose to eat the very substance that causes harm explored. Discourses of risk and pleasure emerge as individuals make choices regarding how to live with various levels of risk and reward. I also explore how those in a variety of communities map (and remember) those who have died as a result of various levels of violence. I end the chapter thinking about what types of violence are remembered (and prevented).

Own Worst Enemy

The April 13, 2012, episode of the public radio show *This American Life*, titled "Own Worst Enemy," features stories about people who "can't stop getting in their own way." The prologue describes how various people with allergies and food sensitivities eat food that will make them feel terrible and might even send them to the hospital. Dan Blumberg, a former employee at WBEZ Chicago, a public radio station, comes to work one day with a swollen face and "cauliflower ears." Apparently Blumberg is allergic to crab, which he loves, but only one out of three times that he eats the allergen will he "turn into, like, the Stay Puft Marshmallow Man." Blumberg thinks it was "the eyes" that "would have been freaking people out" with a "sunken look." This particular episode was his "wake up call," causing him to decide that he wouldn't eat crab (or lobster, another allergen) without first taking a Benadryl "as a sort of aperitif" while carrying his inhaler and injectable epinephrine.[3]

An aperitif is an alcoholic drink, like champagne or gin, that is consumed before a meal to stimulate the appetite. It is meant to be pleasing to the palate and to prepare the diner for the rest of the meal. An hors d'oeuvre or amuse-bouche serves the same purpose. These small bites (or drinks) prepare the diner to take in, enjoy, and later digest the meal. In Blumberg's narrative, the antihistamine pill (diphenhydramine, also known by the brand name Benadryl) acts as a key to open and prepare the stomach to receive the allergen, which is well loved by Blumberg. Unlike most aperitifs, Benadryl is sharp and bitter and frankly not pleasing to taste, although most people swallow the pill without tasting it. But the bitter flavor is part of what enables

Blumberg to later enjoy the crustacean. The antihistamine is a type of in-surance against a more severe reaction; it may stave off something poten-tially life threatening.

In her memoir, *Don't Kill the Birthday Girl,* Sandra Beasley writes about Benadryl: "I knew what it tasted like (nothing at all), how easily one went down, how quickly another four or five could go down, how it made my eyelids sweetly heavy within a half hour. To an anxious and sleep-starved teenager attending a high-pressure high school, that didn't sound like such a bad way to go. At times that sounded like heaven." A few paragraphs later she writes, "I used to wonder if I was the only one tempted to overdose. As I grew older and began meeting other people with allergies, we would crack wise on our membership in the cult of Benadryl carriers. There is no diplomatic way of asking, 'So, did you ever think about taking a whole handful at once?'"[4] Blumberg doesn't de-scribe the same type of relationship with Benadryl that Beasley describes, wherein she reflects on her "anxious" and "sleep-starved" teenage self, but I bring the two discourses of taking Benadryl together to illustrate how this tiny pink pill, which can be widely available (and relatively cheap, especially ge-neric versions), serves many purposes for allergic individuals beyond just pre-venting symptoms of allergic reaction (or motion sickness or cold symptoms).[5] Somewhere in the mix of overdosing, coping with stress, ableism, and "taking as needed," an allergic person's relationship with an antihistamine allows for a type of usage pattern that facilitates the taking of risks, even if others fail to understand these choices. As Glabau writes:

> Food allergy is peculiar among modern diseases because the pa-tient's memory and the real-time functions of their body are often considered more reliable than the way the body is mediated through modern medicine's sophisticated technological apparatus. Much of modern biomedical practice makes a habit of suspending belief in a patient's symptoms until it can be technologically verified, whether through a 19th century technology like a stethoscope or a computer-ized CT scanner. How can a disease be "real" in the 21st century if it cannot be validated by laboratory techniques that operate indepen-dently of human bodies?[6]

Indeed, part of the discourse that emerges in this chapter is a realization that for some allergic individuals, the "real-time functions" of their bodies are un-derstood and anticipated, despite what can be verified via medical science. An individual might be able to eat crab once a year without a reaction, but com-bining crab with alcohol might increase the risk of a reaction. Of course, none of this might be verifiable via lab tests.

As part of the episode of *This American Life*, in his exchange with host Ira Glass, Blumberg discusses his choice to eat crab twice a year. He also acknowledges that his doctor doesn't know about his secret crab meals (although his choice to be on national public radio might have made it harder to maintain the secrecy). He remarks, "I get sleepy from the Benadryl. That's the worst part; I get really tired." Sleepiness isn't the only reaction, though, for the individuals featured in the radio segment. Another person on the episode, Ruthie Zinchuck, is lactose intolerant, but she loves pizza. When she eats pizza, she has "severe stomach cramping. And I'll have to go to the bathroom like immediately. It's no joke." Intolerance is not an allergy, although both types of reactions can make the individual feel very sick. Zinchuck's "no joke" illustrates this point as she hints to terrible gastrointestinal problems as a result of eating pizza. Still, she mentions that it is her "go-to" meal when she doesn't know what to eat. (She doesn't say whether she takes a pill that helps her digest the lactose.) She eats pizza twice a week despite the guarantee of an immediate trip to the bathroom. The appeal and taste of pizza are too great for her to turn the food down.

On the same episode, Elsie Hagisfeld discusses how various members of her family, including her, eat the foods they are allergic to, such as citrus and tomatoes. Hagisfeld remarks, "I don't know if I have any great stories about it because we just do it all the time. We apparently are a family that has absolutely no self-control or good sense. I'm not sure which, but whatever. I like it!" I'm struck by her declaration at the end: "I like it!" Despite negative bodily reactions and possibly death, she presumably loves both the taste of these foods and the risks they present. She manages the hives and itchiness in order to continue to eat items that causes allergic reactions. Diarrhea, stomach pain, swollen eyes, itchiness, hives—and even the risk of anaphylaxis—are managed or tolerated for bites of pizza, lobster, and pineapple.[7] And while the stories may make an interesting segment in a radio show about self-sabotage or people who "can't stop getting in their own way," the segment ends with a brief exchange between host Ira Glass and emergency room doctor Michelle DeVito about the frequency with which individuals come to the ER after having eaten allergens, to illustrate the seriousness of certain allergic reactions. The episode quickly moves on to individuals who eat steak that gets stuck in their narrowed esophagus, and then to a more general discussion of "bad choices" people make. It employs a moral tone, using phrases like "out-of-control diabetic" and describing sending text messages while driving.

This discussion of allergic reactions as resulting from "bad choices" or being "out of control" comes from a conception that management of disease or disability requires submission to standard protocols of medical advice, including avoidance, abstention, and prescription drug compliance. For many, a diagnosis of food allergy (or diabetes, for example) means that the individual will follow the advice to avoid certain foods and always carry the prescribed medicine. For others, the desire to consume more risky foods—and to choose pleasure before safety—means that certain off-limit foods are back on their plates. My favorite foods are only produced in kitchens full of nuts, and each time I reach for those foods I am taking a risk. But I would rather eat the foods and manage my risk exposure as much as I can than be limited to eating foods produced in allergy-safe kitchens and factories. I would choose my favorite foods if they were made in an allergen-free kitchen and widely available everywhere. Both modes of negotiation require varying levels of economic privilege, legal requirement, urban location, and cultural capital. For example, Barbara Melman, another individual featured in *This American Life*, connected stomach pain, nausea, and trips to the emergency room to eating nuts, popcorn, and trail mix. After eliminating them from her diet for a period of time, she started eating them again. In her exchange with Glass, she mentions how her hotel room is full of these items. Glass asks, "Wait, don't you think you're playing with fire?"

> MELMAN: Well, you know, it's not going to kill me. And if it does, I guess I won't know. It won't kill me. No, I mean, it's throwing up. It's not like I have to go through surgery.
> GLASS: Just a quick trip to the hospital, an IV, some medication.
> MELMAN: A few hours, mm-hm. And meet some nice people and leave.

If you remove the details about the hospital and treatment, Melman's last remark sounds like she is meeting friends as opposed to visiting the emergency room in pain: Spend a bit of time, get acquainted with some nice people, and then go back home. In her management of food and embodiment, Melman decides to eat foods that can send her to the emergency room. It is a choice that many make despite others trying to vilify or pathologize them. The "out-of-control" label attempts to assure listeners that people making these choices are being irresponsible, dangerous, or even harmful to themselves and also burdening the health care system. Are there ways beyond moral blame in which the experiences of individuals who make these choices can be represented? At what point does the risk outweigh the benefits?

My intent in this chapter is not to simply affirm or vilify these individuals for the choices they make. Rather, I consider these narratives to expand on the various choices (and allergic calculations), and to highlight how desire, pleasure, taste, and risk can be intertwined. It should not come as a surprise that people do things they "ought not" or "should not" do. If eating a Bakewell tart will trigger anaphylaxis, many people will not eat the tart. But if it causes stomach discomfort or hives, perhaps they might. If these reactions appear only one out of every three times the tart is consumed, then one might choose to eat the tart more frequently. What choice might a person make if anaphylaxis could occur one in ten times, or one in three? Other factors—such as the age of the individual, access to health insurance, and the availability of medical care—might impact the choice.

I'm reminded of a time when I was a counselor at a sleepover summer camp. One night for dinner, vegetables with pesto sauce were served. I knew that pesto often contained pine nuts, but I did not realize that the vegetables were coated in pesto. I loaded my plate and started eating. Almost immediately I realized that I had eaten nuts when my throat tingled and my airway began to constrict. What I "should" have done at that moment was use the epinephrine injector I "should" have been carrying with me, and then ask the staff to call an ambulance or rush me to the emergency room for further treatment. I did not do any of those things. My epinephrine was back in my cabin, so I quickly excused myself from the table by saying I had to use the bathroom. I ran to my cabin and stabbed my thigh with the injector. Immediately my throat opened back up, and the tingle dissipated. I reached for my bottle of antihistamines, took out three or four pills, and swallowed them without any water. I walked back to dinner, took my seat, and ate around the vegetables. That night I took more Benadryl before falling asleep. It was not until years later that I realized how many "mistakes" I had made that night and how seemingly lucky I was to have woken up the next morning.

If experience is a lesson, I learned that allergens might not always be visible. I also learned that pine nuts (along with Brazil nuts) can cause me to have an almost immediate and serious reaction. I was reminded again of the need to communicate my allergies to the kitchen staff and to inquire if a particular item contains an allergen. There have been other times when I have narrowly avoided eating pine nuts. One was when I forgot to have my injectable epinephrine with me, and instead of being a short run back to the cabin it was an hour-long car ride away.

I have eaten something I was allergic to on multiple occasions. *You ate what?* (Pesto, pesto, pesto, rice with pine nuts, cookies with pecans.) *Why?* (I was told it was safe; I didn't realize it contained nuts; it was an accident; I didn't pay attention; I wanted to eat it.) *Did you take a shot?* (No, I forgot to have my injector on me.) *Did you go to the hospital?* (No, I couldn't afford the emergency room visit.) *You should have known better.* The interrogation goes on.

The moral blame lodged at those who intentionally ingest food that makes them sick is not separate from the blame for those who are endangered by lack of clear information or lack of options. At any point, sick and disabled people can be blamed for not doing the "right" things or desiring the wrong things. Requiring care after sickness is framed as an inconvenience. Instead of seeing Hae-rin's cucumber soju as merely a plot device meant to signal her irrationality and point to viewers that she is an unsuitable romantic partner for the charismatic male lead, I want to recognize her choice to drink what makes her sick as an understandable and even desirable way of being. Whatever we eat and do in the world need not be done to improve heath or to avoid sickness, disability, and death.

Hairy Vine, No Friend of Mine

While writing part of this book, I was living in Seoul on research leave from the university. The apartment I rented was down the street from a very popular chicken soup restaurant. Regardless of the weather, during the lunch rush dozens of people would line up waiting to enter the shop. I walked past the restaurant almost daily not knowing that otdak is also served there. Otdak (옻닭), which might be translated as lacquer tree chicken soup, or sumac chicken soup, is similar to another popular Korean dish, samgyetang (삼계탕), which is boiled chicken soup with ginseng. Other herbs, garlic, dried fruit, and nuts are often added as well. Samgyetang is believed to increase overall health, especially during the hottest days of summer. Otdak is eaten to improve health because of the presence of lacquer tree branches, but eating the soup can also cause an allergic reaction of hives, a rash, or internal inflammation.

On the English version of the restaurant's menu, the dish is recommended for those with weak qi (low energy) or a weak stomach, after drinking, or for general pain relief.[8] Under the description of the soup is a note to avoid the soup if you have a sumac allergy. I never did eat the soup at the restaurant, but I did ask many people if they had an allergic reaction while eating it. My random sampling of acquaintances illustrated that eating the soup without a reaction was a source of a bit of pride or accomplishment. I did not come across anyone who ate the soup on a regular basis and still had to take antihistamines or steroid pills to manage (or prevent) a reaction. Some restaurants offer antihistamine pills with the soup. Articles in medical journals state that some people eat the soup risking the reaction, and others eat the soup to balance its purported health and nutritional benefits with the allergic reaction it triggers.[9]

Rhymes like "Hairy vine, no friend of mine" remind people of the itchy potential of poison ivy. A chance (or accidental) encounter with poison ivy, oak, or sumac will result in an incredibly itchy rash that will last two to three weeks. At home, self-care is the recommended course of treatment, with advice to soak in an oatmeal bath, take over-the-counter antihistamines, and avoid scratching offered as tips for enduring the reaction. "Leaves of three, let it be" is another reminder to avoid the pain and inconvenience of the allergic reaction associated with urushiol, the oily allergenic compound found in poison ivy and other members of the Anacardiaceae family. Contact with urushiol causes dermatitis in those allergic to the substance; it rarely causes anaphylaxis, more often a rash and blisters. Urushiol is used in lacquerware in Korea, Japan, and China, and artisans are often subject to allergic reactions as part of the labor connected to making the products. *Toxicodendron vernicifluum*, or the Chinese, Japanese, or Korean lacquer tree, provides the vital ingredient to make the lacquerware, which is also used in traditional herbal remedies for stomach ailments, coughs, liver conditions, and inflammation. Studies are ongoing to determine the effectiveness of the lacquer tree's bark or sap in treating various cancers. Managing exposure to urushiol is a challenge in these treatments. One inventive approach includes using mushrooms to detoxify the bark and remove the urushiol.[10]

Jina Lyu, of the food blog *Yum Korea*, begins her posting about otdak chicken soup with the following, "I might be the first blogger to write about Otdak." Indeed, while Korean-language postings about otdak soup are plentiful, Lyu's posting is one of the few references in English—outside medical studies like those cited above—addressing how to control for the allergenic properties of urushiol in food and medicinal preparations. One medical study discusses a case of a twenty-year-old that went to an emergency room with facial edema and a body rash days after eating otdak. The individual was diagnosed with minimal change disease (MCD), which is a kidney disease resulting in higher amounts of protein in the urine.[11] Individuals with MCD are often given a course of steroids, resulting in complete remission.

Lyu writes, "When you eat it first, you need to take a medicine which prevents you from rashes. Some people always need to take medicine before eating Otdak and others do not. I took medicine for the first couple times and then quit taking it and I was fine. It depends on the individual." In a 2012 article in *Annals of Dermatology*, Jung Eun Kim and colleagues argue for the banning of foods containing lacquer in South Korea. The authors review thirty-three cases of systemic contact dermatitis (SCD) at Soonchunhyang University Hospital in Cheonan during a six-month period. Most cases resulted from eating either otdak or lacquer tree sprouts. In particular, in Chungnam province eating spring lacquer shoots is a widespread practice. A majority of the patients presented with generalized maculopapular rash, a type of red rash with small bumps.[12]

The article includes a headless shot of a torso with the rash covering a significant part of the individual's stomach, chest, and upper arms. These types of images are not uncommon in medical journals, as the documentation of the rash provides evidence of the allergic reaction. As a disability studies scholar, I am reminded of eugenic (and/or medical textbook) images of disabled bodies, often with a black box covering the individual's eyes. These bodies were photographed or displayed to teach about disability or to argue for eugenic state control. While the torso in this image is not part of some effort to argue for sterilization, I do find the pairing of images with the desire to ban all food products containing lacquer to be a use of signs of bodily pain (inconvenience) that the larger food allergy blogging community has not engaged in. Images of rashes, bodies covered in hives, or epinephrine injection marks on thighs are not shared to argue for increased medical coverage or food production safety. Of course, this would be a delicate (and risky) strategy, as disabled (and fat, nonwhite, and noncisgender male) bodies are already always on display. The violences enacted against a multiplicity of bodies that are wrongly assumed to be too _____ (queer, dark, fat, hairy, disabled, foreign) enacts a heavy toll that can result in pain and premature death.

Urushiol is also connected to a Japanese Shingon Buddhist practice known as sokushinbutsu, which involves self-mummification, or "a Buddha in this very body." The process takes at minimum three years to complete and was made illegal in 1877 by the Meiji government. To begin, a monk practiced mokujikigyō, which translates to "tree-eating training." The monk would eat whatever substance could be found in his mountain habitat, including nuts, berries, roots, tree bark, and pine needles, for a thousand days. This was done to rid the body of fat and muscle, but also to "toughen the spirit and distance oneself from the common human world." The practice also prevented the production of bacteria and postdeath decomposition. Once ready, the monk would stop eating all food, drinking only saltwater for a hundred days. It is also believed that the monks would drink tea made from the lacquer tree, which contains urushiol. The tea made the body "less hospitable to the bacteria and parasites that aid in decomposition." While still alive the monk was buried in a box below ground to meditate and prepare for death. An airhole with a bamboo "straw" inserted through it connected the monk to the disciples aboveground. If the monk failed to ring a bell at preset intervals, the disciples assumed the monk had passed away and sealed the tomb. After a thousand days, the tomb was opened, and if the corpse had not decomposed the monk became an "instant Buddha." In an article in the *Japan Times*, author Alex Martin interviewed his cousin, Nobuhiko Takayama, who recalled taking regular family outings to visit the mummified corpses at temples. Takayama called it a "strange choice for a family outing," but according to Martin many of the corpses are connected to fascinating stories, which still bring people to the temples.[13]

For some people, drinking tea or eating foods containing urushiol, despite it being a substance that triggers hives, rashes, and discomfort, allows for spiritual preparation, increased health, and renewal, even while they risk allergic reaction or participate in a ritual to prepare them for a religiously inspired death. The saying "Berries white, run in flight" warns individuals to avoid plants like poison ivy, but despite such warnings, at least for the anticipated future, otdak will remain on menus in restaurants in South Korea, and emergency room doctors will continue to treat individuals for SCD and related conditions brought on by urushiol. I focus on otdak and other plants containing urushiol because they offer a clear example of how individuals make choices to balance risk, taste, and pleasure with a desire to be spontaneous. Even if a person becomes sick, the complex meanings behind these dishes and practices mean that moralizing and restrictions do not work. This section reinforces my assertion that food allergy activists can argue for increased access to injectable epinephrine, allergy-safe foods, and allergy testing while refusing to participate in the vilification of and ableist moralizing against sick and disabled people.

Thinking Through (and Mapping) Death

A thirteen-year-old male respondent to a study about teenage experiences of food allergy reports, "Well because I've had it since I was little I've always known what I can and can't have . . . there have been occasions where I've bought a chocolate bar . . . I've thought 'Ooh I've never had that before,' and I've looked on the back, after I've taken a couple of bites, and it says hazelnuts or almonds and I think, 'Well nothing's happened so far.' So I take the risk."[14] It is assumed that teenagers take unnecessary risks. This particular individual is described in the study as being part of a smaller subset that tolerates risk well. He makes "riskier" eating choices, including eating a chocolate bar without checking the ingredients first. Within studies of food allergy, a small subset of literature explores the reasons why teenagers do not follow treatment protocol in managing their food allergies. Some teenagers apparently do not carry their injectable epinephrine or frequently/accidentally/sometimes eat food containing allergens. In two studies, a significant number of teenagers have "knowingly eaten food containing their allergen."[15] Sometimes the teens eat a small amount of food to determine the presences of allergens, especially if the ingredients are unknown. Some individuals practice the "eat and wait" type of allergy management. In the study by Sampson and colleagues, the various reasons for eating the allergenic food include "it looked good and I wanted to eat it," "did not want to ask about ingredients," "hanging out with friends," "testing to see if still allergic," and "all my friends were eating the food." The overall motivations varied, but participants listed multiple reasons for practicing this type of allergy management. It is important to note that sometimes the motivation was due to the practices of peers, while at other times the food looked too delicious not to eat. These teenagers are making choices regarding eating and allergy management, even if the choices are assumed to be risky or dangerous. A common response to such behavior is to encourage teens to avoid allergens and to carry the appropriate medication at all times. Interestingly, a group of researchers is working on wearable epinephrine injectors to potentially limit risk to teenagers. I discuss these in the Introduction to the book.

In *Chronic Youth*, Julie Passanante Elman writes that during the 1990s, known as the "Decade of the Brain," "scientific knowledge about the brain permeated popular culture, [and] representations of 'crazy' teenagers with dangerous (and endangered) incomplete brains manifested a new image of adolescence as a form of temporary 'brain damage' that required new forms of rehabilitative management." Elman argues that focusing on individual brains (and personal will) as a solution to violence, drug use, and school violence meant that structural inequalities were exacerbated as teens became "a species, characterized by biological risk factors." As a result, "teens became patients with treatment options."[16] But this focus on treatment can fail to account for why some teenagers cannot or do not do what medical authorities ask them to do. From encouraging teens to avoid using drugs or abstain from sexual activity, to telling them to always carry epinephrine, there is a long genealogy of efforts to modify teenager behavior. Many times, these efforts fail to achieve the intended outcome. Individualizing the responsibility for safe food consumption and thinking about this failure as individual teenagers' noncompliance erases the forces of poverty, racism, and other structural inequalities that constrain choice. Advocacy for widespread injectable epinephrine in public spaces, robust labeling and sanitization practices in kitchens and factories, and expanded access to allergy-safe foods, especially for impoverished individuals, might do more to prevent accidental death than focusing on individual solutions to systemic problems.

Regrettably, there are cases where an individual accidentally eats an allergen and dies because of an allergic reaction. In the United States, a handful of these cases occur annually. Food allergy blogs and websites, like No Nut Traveler, and magazines, like *Allergic Living*, share news of these tragedies, which prompts expressions of sympathy and concern and increased regulation

of labeling or of airlines. Many of the stories involve an individual, usually a
child or teenager, who ate something without knowing that it contained the
allergen (rather than knowingly taking a risk). Consider the situation where
the allergic reaction is quite severe and access to injectable epinephrine is not
ensured. In other cases, an individual receives an injection (or two) of epinephrine before being transported to a hospital, but they still enter a coma and
ultimately die. Sometimes fatal allergic reactions are unexpected because an
individual's previous reaction to an allergen was minor. In these cases, epinephrine might not have been prescribed. Moreover, parents and allergic individuals are sometimes unsure how to use injectable epinephrine, or they fail to fill
their prescription.[17]

Fifteen-year-old Natasha Ednan-Laperouse ate a baguette sandwich at a
Heathrow Airport branch of Pret a Manger before boarding a flight with her
father bound to Nice, France. The sandwich was freshly made at the store (as
opposed to being made and wrapped off-site) and was not labeled with any
allergen information. Ednan-Laperouse had an allergy to sesame. Although
the bread contained sesame, an allergen-labeling policy exemption existed for
food prepared daily on-site. Despite her father administering two doses of injectable epinephrine, the teenager passed away in a French hospital. An inquest revealed that the brand of injector the father used had needles that were
16 millimeters (mm) in length and contained 300 micrograms (mcg) of adrenaline. Adequate dosing requires a needle length of 25 mm and 500 mcg of
adrenaline.[18] A study from 2014 documents that in 19 percent of adults and
28 percent of women, the needle length in the most frequently used epinephrine injector was insufficient. That said, in Ednan-Laperouse's case, a 2018
response to the coroner's inquest finding challenged the assertion about insufficient needle length. One brand of injector available in some parts of Europe
advertises that it has longer needles than its competitors. Another study concludes that depending on body size, there is a risk of children injecting the
epinephrine into bone, or of adults not reaching muscle.[19]

As a result of the inquest, Pret a Manger agreed to provide labeling for products made fresh at its stores, despite not being legally required to do so. During the year prior to Ednan-Laperouse's death, there were twenty-one cases of
allergic reaction at Pret a Manger locations in the UK. Unfortunately, the tragic
death of Ednan-Laperouse follows a similar pattern. Individuals accidentally
eat foods containing allergens, often because either the person assumes that
the item does not contain the allergen, or they do not tell the kitchen or waitstaff about their allergy. To be sure, communication does not prevent all accidental allergic reactions, as evidenced by a case at Panera in which a mother
specifically asked for a grilled cheese sandwich for her daughter to be made

free from peanut butter. Yet the sandwich was made with peanut butter, and after the child took a bite she was rushed to the emergency room. The case is currently being litigated in Massachusetts.[20] For many, the best approach involves communicating about allergies multiple times to both waitstaff and chefs, while also researching online menus and allergy guides. This approach takes planning and access to information that can be clearly understood. Further, as I have argued in this chapter, the individualized approach continues to frame food allergy management as a personal health issue and not a societal responsibility that requires expanded access to allergen-free food, medicine, and health care.

The National Food Death Allergy Registry (NFDAR) is an online-based archive that records the stories of individuals in the United States who died as a result of accidental ingestion of allergens. NFDAR lists only the age of the individual, their initials, and the location where they died. Other information is added after the family consents, but gender and racial status are mostly not listed. The registry is a project of Stacy Dorris, a pediatric allergist and immunologist located in Nashville, Tennessee. Dorris cites a personal connection to the project, as her daughter is allergic to peanuts and her brother has food allergies. In an interview with the Allergy and Asthma Network, Dorris remarked, "I want to support the data with clinical facts. The more information we have, the better we'll be able to understand why food allergy deaths occur and how to prevent them in the future." The project includes a map "that vividly illustrated where individuals have lost their lives throughout the United States due to food allergies."[21]

Dorris tells the story of Anthony L., who passed away in July 2017. Anthony L. ate three-fourths of an energy bar that contained nuts before his friends let him know about the nuts. He was not carrying his autoinjector. His friends took him to the hospital, but he died on the way.[22] This tragic death serves as a reminder of the necessity to read labels and carry injectable epinephrine. Another story, from 1983, relates that "CH" passed away at the age of twenty-three after eating seafood. An overwhelming majority of the people catalogued on the website died before age twenty. The list acts also as a testimony to the failures of a health care system that individualizes food allergy management instead of demanding publicly available and subsidized injectable epinephrine, robust food allergy labeling laws, and widespread access to safe food.

There are similar lists of allergy-related deaths that move beyond the borders of the United States. Lisa Rutter of No Nuts Moms Group maintains a list on her blog. She also links to articles that report on the deaths of the individuals. Unlike NFADR, the No Nuts Moms Group has a comments feature where it is not uncommon for family members or friends to express appreciation to Rutter for remembering their loved one. One particular posting caught my attention. A mother, Kari, wrote to ask that her son Cody be added to the list: "My son Cody passed away from anaphylactic shock November 21st 2013. He had a milk allergy; he was trying to increase his tolerance to milk and secretly drank 16 ounces of strawberry milk out at a park by himself at night. He died at the park from aphixiation [sic]." The NFADR has a fuller account of Cody's life, indicating that he was seventeen when he passed away. The teenager, who hoped to outgrow his allergies, tried to "desensitize" his system by consuming milk, including a sandwich sauce that contained milk. The NFADR post also mentions that in fourth grade, Cody had a reaction to a bean and cheese burrito at school. He wanted to eat the burrito to "be like the other kids." On the night when he drank the strawberry milk, Cody was alone in the park. I can only imagine how frightening it must have been to be alone while having trouble breathing and communicating to the 911 operator, and ultimately dying as a result of asphyxiating on his own vomit. That night, Cody was not carrying his inhaler (for his asthma) or his autoinjector.[23] His desire to be like others without allergies illustrates how challenging it can be for teenagers in particular to fit in when difference can result in bullying and ostracization. Thinking about Cody's story makes me wonder how many individuals with food allergies are privately trying to desensitize themselves to their allergens without being connected to a community of support and without having robust access to allergy testing and treatment and allergen-safe food.

The map (and index) of death connects to other efforts to visually connect how (and when) other communities experience/are affected by early (and often violent) death. Mapping Police Violence, for example, helps to visualize the number of people killed by police in the United States, including the disproportionate number of BIPOC individuals murdered by police. The website documents the ways in which Black people are more likely than their white counterparts to be killed, and shows that in forty-seven of the fifty largest cities in the country, police kill Black people at higher rates than they do white people. When logging on to the website, the viewer sees a dynamic map rapidly loading markers on a map of the United States. Each point on the map documents an individual being killed by the police. Visitors to the site can click on a point on the map to learn more about the individual case. The team behind the website writes, "We cannot wait to know the true scale of police violence against our communities. In a country where at least three people are killed by police every day, we cannot wait for police departments to provide us with these answers. The maps and charts on this site aim to provide us with some insights into patterns of police violence across the country."[24] They continue, "We hope these data will be used to provide greater transparency and accountability for police departments as part of the ongoing campaign to end police violence in our communities." An important distinction between this website and the ones discussed above is the focus on systemic oppression directly tied to white supremacy. Deaths of individuals due to allergies are not visibly connected on those websites to lack of medical care exacerbated by poverty, out-of-pocket expenses, or limited access to testing. There is no discussion about how an individual's social identities, including race and gender, might have expedited their death. Beyond calling for more robust allergen-labeling policies, which are critically important but not sufficient to prevent all deaths, these remembrances of death connect the person with allergies to a family that remembers and mourns them.

Another effort at mapping death linked to structural oppression and criminalization of migration tries to visualize the deaths of migrants, which often happen in deserted locations. Humane Borders, in partnership with the Pima County Medical Examiner's Office, maintains a migrant death map that documents where migrants' bodies were found along the border between the United States and Mexico. Humane Borders "maintains a system of water stations in the Sonoran Desert on routes used by migrants" in order to help "create a just and humane environment in the borderlands." The mapping project allows users to search the results using a variety of terms, including name, gender, year of death, and cause of death.[25] In early June 2019, when I first drafted this section of the chapter, the latest bodies that had been found were skeletal remains with some ligaments attached. The medical examiner's office estimated these remains to be three months postmortem. However, for the two sets of remains found on May 30, 2019, there is not any information (other than gender for one of the bodies), illustrating that these deaths are often cruel and that it can take months before remains are found. Families and communities are probably wondering what happened to their loved ones as the individual quite literally decomposes in the Arizona desert. I find myself wondering what material conditions expedited these deaths. How did a lack of water and food, including perhaps allergen-free food, mean that these migrants suffered alone in the desert? All of us committed to food allergy activism should partner with Black Lives Matter, prison-abolition activists, and migration-justice activists to demand an end to policies and practices that result in these early and violent deaths of individuals of color.

What is also missing in these stories of allergic-related death is an analysis of how structural inequalities, peer pressure, or other social forces constrained choice or meant that the individual died. Many of the more publicly known individuals are white or light skinned, further erasing the impact of food allergy across racial and ethnic categories. As a scholar committed to extending an analysis of how interlocking systems of oppression manifest themselves, I want to push this conversation of death and allergy beyond the tragic deaths of (white) teenagers. Here I am asking all of us to consider which deaths we do not have information about, and to demand information about how allergies are managed in immigration facilities, group homes, prisons, refugee camps, and other institutions. How can we extend our food allergy activism beyond schools and pantries to other spaces, where people are incarcerated or constrained by white supremacy, racialized capitalism, and inhumane migration policies? Responding to the invitation extended by Emily Brown in her open letter, I repeat that we need to connect our work of food allergy activism to Black Lives Matter and racial justice efforts to address the ways in which white supremacy and anti-Blackness continue to result in early and violent death.

There has been limited effort to address food allergies in prisons. Jamie Longazel and Rachel Archer wrote "The Inadequacy of Prison Food Allergy Policies" to discuss the fact that which state an individual is incarcerated in can mean that their access to testing and allergen-free food is severely limited. They point out that there is no reliable data about food allergies in prison. The authors do not take an abolitionist approach; rather they seek to reform prison management of food allergies. I disagree that prisons can be reformed. We need to abolish prisons and carceral spaces. As Mariame Kaba argues, "While some offer calls for reform, such calls ignore the reality that an institution grounded in the commodification of human beings, through torture and the deprivation of their liberty cannot be made good. The logic of using policing, punishment, and prison has not proven to address the systemic causes of violence."[26]

Likewise, I could not find any information about how food allergies are managed in other spaces, like migration or refugee camps. Unlike journalistic accounts and food allergy blogs discussing food allergy plans and laws in schools, summer camps, airplanes, and dorm rooms, which tend to impact white allergic individuals in greater numbers, there is almost nothing about how institutionalized and incarcerated folks, including many BIPOC individuals with allergies and other disabilities, are impacted by limited access to safe food, testing, or accommodations. As I argue in this book, food allergy impacts all communities, and a robust coalition can work together to advance the demands of racial justice, disability justice, and food justice while centering BIPOC communities.

I did locate the story of Michael Saffioti, who died while incarcerated in the Snohomish County Jail, in Washington State, because of an allergic reaction. Despite communicating his dairy allergy to the staff, and having it documented, he was served and ate oatmeal that contained dairy. After repeatedly asking to visit the nurse, he was forced to stay in his cell, where he was found dead. *Allergic Living* published three articles about his death and about a lawsuit that Saffioti's family filed afterward (which was settled). One of the articles mentions that Saffioti used marijuana to manage stress and anxiety around his food allergy and asthma; he had been arrested for marijuana possession.[27] Saffioti is light skinned, and the journalistic accounts report on his family and attachment to community, which makes him relatable to the readers of the magazine. I bring this up to highlight how the only case I could find about an incarcerated individual dying because of an allergic reaction involves another young, seemingly white person that was incarcerated with a misdemeanor. Like the other deaths, Saffioti's is tragic and should have been prevented, but as food-allergic activists we need to examine the larger structures that confine and restrict, especially the prison system, which incarcerates an overwhelming number of BIPOC individuals by utilizing racist and ableist policing. Instead of just arguing for greater access to food allergy testing or safe foods, we should join prison abolitionists to demand the closing of carceral spaces in exchange for greater investment in communities of color, including investment in sustainable health and food systems.

Unlike the often very public remembrances of some who died because of accidental ingestion of allergens, the circumstances of death for others in spaces like prisons, detention camps, and group homes are underreported or not disclosed at all. Also rarely reported are the deaths of those that intentionally consumed allergens. I want to be clear that I am not saying that one version of grief or remembrance is more valid than the other. Nor am I arguing that the methods used by food allergy bloggers and community members to raise awareness of the deaths of individuals are not effective. Rather, when an individual dies from an allergic reaction, like Natasha Ednan-Laperouse, who is light skinned, multiple remembrances and blog posts appear alongside newspaper and journalistic accounts. The silences around the deaths of certain people, including those that are multiply disabled or migrants of color, help to hide the forces of violence and oppression that communities face. The (white) teenager/child who dies from hidden dairy or soy becomes a tragedy because it is unexpected and interrupts their assumed (re)productive future. They are often remembered in relation to their family members—and memorialized as such. But a migrant of color who dies because of dehydration and lack of food is not reported on as someone who was connected to a community. Prisoners who die in prison are assumed to be criminal. The "severely" disabled individual murdered by a caregiver, or the undocumented migrant of color who dies is assumed to lack a future (or a life) to protect or mourn. As Alison Kafer remarks, "A better future, in other words, is one that excludes disability and disabled bodies; indeed it is the very *absence* of disability that signals this better future."[28] This celebrated future is also devoid of discussions about dismantling white supremacy, opening borders, and enabling individuals to self-determine their own futures, families, loves, and lives. Broadening conceptions of the future beyond a capitalist formulation of white, cisgender, heteronormative, and ableist families shifts the focus regarding which violence and deaths ought to be prevented or mourned.

I began this chapter by discussing the representations of individuals who choose to eat food that is potentially dangerous. I sought to discuss individuals who regularly eat allergens and manage their symptoms to flush out deeper connections between risk, desire, pleasure, and safety. In doing so, though, I was continuously reminded that death is not preventable. And that only certain deaths are assumed to be "tragic." I end this chapter with an urgent call to expand the focus beyond the handful of allergic deaths that are reported (and reposted) each year. Expanding the focus to include a discussion of how multiple communities experience violence and death because of a lack of access to health care, including treatments and prescription medicine, shifts the conversation from individual tragedies to larger structural oppressions. The violence against Black disabled people, other disabled people of color, migrants, refugees, those without reliable access to shelter and food, and many other groups affected by structural oppression is connected to the struggle that many severely food-allergic individuals face. The deaths at the border—in cages, camps, deserts, and spaces of incarceration—are deeply connected to the inaccessibility of allergen-free foods and adequate medical care.

Many parents, including Thomas and Dina Silvera, attempt to use their personal tragedy to improve the lives of many more individuals affected by food allergies, especially BIPOC individuals with food allergies. The Silveras' son Elijah Alavi-Silvera passed away after an allergic reaction because of being fed a grilled cheese sandwich at a daycare, despite his documented allergies. As a result of their activism and advocacy, Elijah's Law was signed by New York governor Andrew Cuomo in late 2019. The law requires daycares to implement plans to prevent and treat anaphylactic reactions. The Silveras also advocate for parents to use federal disability laws to create either 504 plans or Individual Education Plans to address their children's food allergies and the need for accommodations. In Ontario, Canada, Sara and Mike Shannon's daughter Sabrina passed away after accidental exposure to dairy in the high school cafeteria. The Shannons lobbied the provincial government to pass Sabrina's Law, which requires school districts to create anaphylaxis plans and individual plans for all students with allergies.[29] Sabrina's Law was the first of its kind in the world and has been the inspiration for many other laws aimed at protecting children with allergies from lethal allergic reactions. These parents are trying to enable futures that are safer for allergic children in school settings. Along with these efforts, as I've stated, food allergy communities should support prison abolition organizations, migrants' rights groups, and racial justice advocates to link food safety, allergies, and health care to a broader agenda that seeks to dismantle white supremacist modes of restriction and incarceration.

In this chapter, I challenge the notion of individual responsibility for risk management and moral blame with regard to the intentional or neglectful ingestion of allergens. I also want to add to the mapping and recording of individual people's deaths an understanding of the social environment of eating, acknowledging that there can be a desire for risky and forbidden food. Allergic people are a diverse group, and our motivations and social capital vary. We cannot consider food allergy a single-identity political issue anymore. Legal requirements, individual behavior management, sympathy, and remembrance are not sufficient to prevent deaths, especially of disabled and poor people of color, without connecting to multiple spaces, including institutions, streets, migrant camps, and prisons, where eating occurs without safety or assurance of survival. Food-allergic communities can move toward a radical agenda of demanding free medical care, including emergency care for all, free epinephrine, and subsidized and readily available allergen-free food. A coalitional group of crip, queer, undocumented, gender diverse, Indigenous, nonwhite people agitating for universal health care (including emergency care for allergic reactions and affordable epinephrine injectors), sustainable housing and food (including foods without allergens), radically welcoming spaces for people with all dietary practices, and the dismantling of carceral spaces—this is the present (and future) that will truly set all free.

Conclusion

Pandemics and the Need for Coalitions

As I boarded a United Airlines flight in June 2021, the flight attendant handed me an alcohol wipe that I could use to clean my seat, seat-back tray, and other surfaces. Scenes like this are repeated daily because surfaces and hands are spots where SARS-CoV-2 can hide. Hand sanitizer is ubiquitous in public locations throughout North America. As I was wiping my seat, I couldn't help thinking about the many allergic individuals, predominantly white individuals with food allergies, who fought for the right to preboard planes so they can do the exact same thing. Removing traces of peanuts, dairy, and other allergens from seats helps mitigate accidental exposure, which helps to calm nervous passengers. In 2019 the United States Department of Transportation (DOT) ruled that American Airlines had violated the Air Carrier Access Act for forbidding an allergic individual from preboarding the flight to wipe down their seat. In their ruling, the DOT linked disability with "severe allergy":

> Section 382.93 states that carriers "must offer preboarding to passengers that self-identify at the gate as needing additional time or assistance to board, stow accessibility equipment, or be seated." Passengers with severe nut allergies are passengers with disabilities for purposes of Part 382. When a passenger with a severe allergy asks for preboarding to wipe down seating surfaces, he or she is requesting additional time "to be seated," because from the passenger's perspective, the seating area cannot be safely accessed until it is wiped down. Accordingly, we have reason to believe that when an airline fails to allow passengers with severe nut allergies to preboard to wipe down seating surfaces, it violates section 382.93.[1]

This effort is incomplete if we focus only on air travel and other spaces of accommodation that center white individuals with food allergies. As I have demonstrated in this book, food allergy—including the planning required to remain safer when exposed to allergens—often requires accommodations from school districts, businesses, friends, and lovers. Yet this work is incomplete unless we also focus on the structural barriers and systems of oppression that do not center the experiences and expertise of disabled people of color. As the COVID-19 pandemic illustrates, in the United States, when disease management is framed as an individual concern and not one of social justice, that means disabled people of color, people living in poverty, and those incarcerated in prisons, institutions, and nursing homes get sick and die regardless of the availability of vaccines and sanitizing agents. When the world remains hostile and dangerous, the food allergic and other disabled people depend on the assistance of others while navigating various levels of risk. In public, there might never be a completely "safe," accessible, or allergen-free location. As disabled people, allergic individuals navigate these choices by making the allergic calculation. Sometimes our choices provide pleasure; at other times we find ourselves in the emergency room.

Disabled individuals sometimes have to make do with what is available, particularly disabled people of color. When unable to afford copays for prescription drugs like injectable epinephrine or insulin, some individuals rely on expired prescriptions or supplies from friends, or they purchase items from non-approved locations. With each option come various levels of risk and precarity. Receiving food assistance from the government and pantries might not always afford "safe" options or enough nutrition for everyone in a household. Individuals make do while still demanding additional levels of support. Resources are pooled and bartered. As Leah Lakshmi Piepzna-Samarasinha writes in her poem "Crip fairy godmother":

> because we write the future with our bodies every day
> that you make it
> and more than you could imagine
> You will gain a wild pack of crips
> sharing vicodin, hearing aid hookups, favorite terps, the shared ramp
> the inside scoop on the lexapro, the link to the beloved breathing
>   mask.[2]

In the middle of exclusion and structural barriers, survival can depend less on insurance approvals and more on the creative connections fostered among communities. Of course, this means that disabled people of color who are incarcerated, institutionalized, and without cultural capital become even more isolated, especially in moments of pandemic. Since the beginnings of the COVID-19 pandemic, disabled people, especially disabled people of color, have often found themselves in situations where access to resources is increasingly compromised, often resulting in their deaths. When health care is rationed and ventilators are in short supply, a racist and ableist health care system will not secure life-sustaining treatments for disabled individuals. Disabled people of color are dying because of institutional settings, lack of access to testing and vaccines, and a rush to return to "normal" when discourses of normal only reify white, able-bodied understandings of sociality and embodiment.

At the same time, modes of connection have facilitated diverse and productively unruly ways of collaborating. Individuals who are usually geographically disconnected can come together to learn, celebrate, and strategize, often using tools of accessibility, including sign language, image descriptions, open captioning, and multilingual translation. Predictably, as universities, organizations, and businesses push for more "in person" programming, classes, and events, the tools that facilitated connections are disappearing. Piepzna-Samarasinha continues:

> Disability is adaptive, interconnected, tenacious, voracious, slutty,
>   silent, raging, life giving
> We are crip Earthseed
> but we are not going anywhere
> You are not an individual health defect
> You are a systemic war battalion
> You come from somewhere
> You are a we
> We know shit they'll need to know
> We know shit they have no idea of
> We have survived a million things they said would kill us
> We prove them all wrong
> Even death is different here
> not a failure
> but a glittery cosmos.[3]

Note the line "You are a we." There are many guesses about how the pandemic will end. Piepzna-Samarasinha is asserting that white, heterosexual, able-bodiedness will assume to know what "success" or "security" will be, yet these conceptions are incomplete and false. Crip survival and crip death remain a "glittery cosmos."

As I was writing and revising this text, I often felt an eerie parallel between various choices allergic individuals and their families make and what the public was being encouraged to do to remain safe from COVID-19. Allergic individuals have been wearing masks on airplanes, wiping down surfaces, not eating in public, frequently washing hands, and negotiating interpersonal exchanges with others when allergens/fluids might be present. It would not be surprising if readers noted these connections as well. While this is explicitly a book about the lives of individuals with food allergies, the insights and texts I incorporate come from a wide range of embodied perspectives and communities.

I end this book excited about the ways in which various food-allergic communities are challenging historical and current practices of exclusion. I am also seeking additional coalitions between racial justice, disability justice, environmental justice, and food allergy activism to be expanded to food justice. As I argue in Chapter 4, a coalition pushing for free health care, sustainable access to food, socially welcoming spaces for all dietary practices, improved access to injectable epinephrine and other prescription drugs, and an end to institutionalization and incarceration can help dismantle systems of oppression and center the lives and experiences of BIPOC disabled people. I am eager for additional cross-community coalitions that demand pleasurable and sustainable presents and futures for all types of bodies, including leaky, fat, queer, racialized, and sick, smelly, and allergic bodies. We cannot wait for government, legislators, and prescription drug companies to address precarity and violence. There remains much work to do to shift our focus from a white allergic experience toward a more representative understanding of the racial, ethnic, religious, and economic diversity of those with food allergies in the United States. As individuals committed to improving the futures of those with food allergies, we should work to dismantle white supremacist, ableist systems that jeopardize the lives of disabled people of color. This is the urgent and necessary work of those with food allergies and their allies.

Acknowledgments

In this book, I have traced the messiness of food allergies and the complicated calculations that those with such allergies make. In doing so, I have also advocated for more robust coalitions, including the advancement of racial and disability justice by food allergy advocates. It is my hope that the readers of this text will find it worthwhile and thought provoking.

I am incredibly grateful to a large group of individuals that supported, challenged, and encouraged me during the many years I spent writing this book. I appreciate the following individuals who read chapters, sometimes in very rough form, and were gracious enough to engage with my work by offering suggestions and productive criticism: Carolyn Lewis, Sara Sanders, Carrie Shanafelt, Anne McGuire, Cynthia Wu, and Kelly Fritsch. Anita Mannur and Alison Kafer read the entire text and offered engaged feedback and invaluable suggestions for revision. I am indebted to them for their generosity during these stressful times that sometimes felt impossible to endure. Their reviews were a precious gift. I also appreciate the anonymous reviewer who provided valuable suggestions for revision. Eunjung Kim is an incredibly generous and discerning reader. She read the entire manuscript and helped me polish my argumentation.

Thank you to Rosanne Mah for your leadership and encouragement. Thank you to Justin Tang for sharing with me about your efforts to create wearable epinephrine. I know medical school is challenging, but I am positive you will be an invaluable advocate for sick and disabled folks of color. Emily Brown is a visionary and a tireless advocate. Thank you for all the work you are doing to link food allergy activism to racial justice.

I thank my family and friends for their encouragement as I worked through this project and also as I have navigated the allergy-management system my entire life. Thank you all for your kindness and support. While I cannot completely repay your generosity, I hope to pass it on to others in the spirit of interdependence.

I presented portions of this text, often in fifteen-minute segments, at conferences and symposiums, including events hosted by the Society for Disability Studies; the National Women's Studies Association; the American Studies Association; Theorising Normalcy and the Mundane; the Global Conference on Food, Heritage, and Community; the Body Fixes Symposium at Northwestern University; and a colloquium in my home department at Syracuse University. I am grateful to the audience members and fellow panelists that listened to my work, gave feedback, and helped me make my arguments more nuanced and fully developed.

Humanities scholars are often managing a few dollars in hopes of being able to afford a conference registration or book purchase. I was fortunate to receive funding from the Grinnell College Committee for Support of Faculty Scholarship and from the School of Education Internal Grant Competition at Syracuse University for supporting travel and book purchases used in preparation of this book.

I am thrilled and fortunate to have worked with Richard Morrison. Richard's editorial skill and imagination enhance any project he works on. I know there are many others at Fordham University Press who worked on my book and whom I will not meet. Thank you all for sharing your skills and expertise.

I love teaching. I often cannot believe that I get to teach amazing students. They trust me to experiment as I try to be a better, more impactful teacher. Thank you to all my current and former students.

I thank all the medical practitioners that have kept me alive when I had a life-threatening allergic reaction. I also thank the emergency room workers, prep cooks, waitstaff, administrators, and many others who took my concerns about allergies and allergic reactions seriously. I am indebted to a fierce and wild group of activists that agitate for safer food, affordable prescription drugs, and better access to testing and treatment. As we continue our work, I am eager for us to expand our efforts to make sure that systemic injustices, including racism and ableism, are addressed.

Notes

Preface

1. Lucy A. Bilaver et al., "Prevalence and Correlates of Food Allergy among Medicaid Enrolled US Children," *Academic Pediatrics* 21, no. 1 (2021): 84–92.

2. In the recently published book *The End of Food Allergy: The First Program to Prevent and Reverse a 21st-Century Epidemic* (New York: Avery, 2020), Kari Nadeau and Sloan Barnett have only one paragraph on "race and ethnicity." Nadeau is the Director of the Sean N. Parker Center for Allergy and Asthma Research at Stanford University, and Barnett is a *New York Times* best-selling author. This text is one of the latest trade publications that offers help and advice for parents of children with food allergies, and for food allergic individuals, attempting to translate the latest scientific discoveries into less technical language. The book is helpful for discussing these discoveries, but it doesn't address structural barriers to treatment and support, thereby failing to challenge white supremacy and structural oppression. *Food without Fear: Identify, Prevent, and Treat Food Allergies, Intolerances, and Sensitivities*, by Ruchi Gupta with Kristin Loberg (New York: Hachette Books, 2021), covers a bit more about the rates of food allergies and access to diagnosis among groups of people. It also discusses Gupta and colleague's 2016 study, which I discuss in the introduction. Yet neither book has a robust discussion about the ways in which allergic individuals of color have negative health outcomes because of structural oppression and limited access to diagnosis, treatment, and allergen-free foods.

3. Mahboobeh Mahdavinia, "Racial Differences in Pediatric Food Allergy," *Physician's Weekly*, March 5, 2019, https://www.physiciansweekly.com/racial -differences-in-pediatric-food-allergy/; Food Equality Initiative, "7 Percent Fund and Coalition," accessed June 26, 2020, https://foodequalityinitiative.networkforgood .com/projects/103093-7-percent-fund-and-coalition (for the sake of transparency,

I will point out that I contribute to this fund quarterly); and Ruchi S. Gupta et al., "The Prevalence, Severity, and Distribution of Childhood Food Allergy in the United States," *Pediatrics* 128, no. 1 (2011): e9–e17.

4. Emily Brown, "Open Letter to the Food Allergy Community," Food Equality Initiative, June 7, 2020, https://foodequalityinitiative.org/open-letter-to-the-food-allergy-community/; Audre Lorde, "An Open Letter to Mary Daly," 1979, History is a Weapon, accessed August 5, 2021, https://www.historyisaweapon.com/defcon1/lordeopenlettertomarydaly.html.

5. Brown, "Open Letter."

6. A YouTube video of the webinar is available here: Food Equality Initiative FEI, "For the Health: Notable Black Voices," video, YouTube, June 26, 2020, https://www.youtube.com/watch?v=2N-tbNmPhnQ. A follow-up conversation recorded a year later is also available here: Food Equality Initiative FEI, "For the Health: Juneteenth Conversation," video, YouTube, June 18, 2021, https://www.youtube.com/watch?v=dYGtpWptahs. The panelists were Emily Brown, Denise Woodard (Partake Foods), Javier Evelyn (Alerje), Dr. Lakia Wright-Bello (Thermo Fisher Scientific), and Thomas and Dina Silvera (Elijah-Alavi Foundation). The event was moderated by Linsey Davis (ABC News correspondent) and Karen Palmer (certified professional coach/operations consultant).

7. Mariam Matti, "Elijah's Law Is Official, Protecting Food Allergy Kids in NY Daycares," *Allergic Living*, September 14, 2019, https://www.allergicliving.com/2019/09/14/elijahs-law-official-protecting-food-allergy-kids-in-ny-daycares/.

8. On social media in early June 2020, many white (or light-skin-appearing) individuals doing food allergy work momentarily signaled "Black Lives Matter," but by the beginning of July 2020 their posts, stories, and podcasts recentered whiteness.

9. Antonello La Vergata, "In the Name of Science: The Conceptual and Ideological Background of Charles Richet's Eugenics," *História, Ciências, Saúde-Manguinhos* 25, suppl. 1 (2018): 125–44, https://doi.org/10.1590/S0104-59702018000300008; Charles Richet, "Anaphylaxis" (Nobel Lecture), December 11, 1913, accessed September 12, 2022, https://www.nobelprize.org/prizes/medicine/1913/richet/lecture/; Nobel Prize, "Charles Richet Biographical," accessed August 13, 2022, https://www.nobelprize.org/prizes/medicine/1913/richet/biographical/.

Introduction: Why Food Allergies?

1. Food Allergy Research and Education, "Facts and Statistics: Key Information to Help Better Understand Food Allergies and Anaphylaxis," accessed August 27, 2022, https://www.foodallergy.org/resources/facts-and-statistics.

2. Mahboobeh Mahdavinia et al., "Racial Differences in Food Allergy Phenotype and Health Care Utilization among US Children," *Journal of Allergy and Clinical Immunology: In Practice* 5, no. 2 (2017): 352–57. This study doesn't use "Latinx," but rather "Hispanic," but in discussing the study later, Gupta uses "Latinx" (*Food without Fear*, 125). I am also using "Latinx" because it is unclear what working

definition the study used for categorization of racial status. In addition, there are multiple critiques of the use of "Hispanic," including the way the United States government has used it to justify imperialism and erase Indigenous identities. Araceli Cruz, "The Problematic History of the Word 'Hispanic,'" *Teen Vogue*, October 9, 2018, https://www.teenvogue.com/story/problematic-history-of-hispanic-word.

3. Corinne A. Keet et al., "Temporal Trends and Racial/Ethnic Disparity in Self-Reported Pediatric Food Allergy in the United States," *Annals of Allergy, Asthma and Immunology* 112, no. 3 (2014): 222–29.

4. Sarah Taylor-Black and Julie Wang, "The Prevalence and Characteristics of Food Allergy in Urban Minority Children," *Annals of Allergy, Asthma and Immunology* 109, no. 6 (2012): 431–37.

5. Ruchi Gupta et al., "The Economic Impact of Childhood Food Allergy in the United States," *JAMA Pediatrics* 167, no. 11 (2013): 1026–31.

6. Ruchi S. Gupta et al., "Prevalence and Severity of Food Allergies among US Adults," *JAMA Network Open* 2, no. 1 (2019): e185630; Alessandro Fiocchi and Vincenzo Fierro, "Food Allergy," World Allergy Organization, March 2017, https://www.worldallergy.org/education-and-programs/education/allergic-disease-resource-center/professionals/food-allergy; Elizabeth Huiwen Tham and Donald Y M Leung, "How Different Parts of the World Provide New Insights into Food Allergy," *Allergy, Asthma and Immunology Research* 10, no. 4 (2018): 290–99.

7. Emily Martin, *Flexible Bodies: Tracking Immunity in American Culture from the Days of Polio to the Age of AIDS* (Boston: Beacon Press, 1994), 101, 109; Mel Y. Chen, *Animacies: Biopolitics, Racial Mattering, and Queer Affect* (Durham, N.C.: Duke University Press, 2012), 194.

8. Stacy Alaimo, *Bodily Natures : Science, Environment, and the Material Self* (Bloomington: Indiana University Press, 2010), 114.

9. Chen, *Animacies*, 7, 10.

10. Moises Velasquez-Manoff, *An Epidemic of Absence: A New Way of Understanding Allergies and Autoimmune Diseases* (New York: Simon and Schuster, 2012), 2, 284; Alexandra Sifferlin, "Doctor Infects Himself with Hookworm for Health Experiment," *Time*, April 18, 2012, https://healthland.time.com/2012/04/18/doctor-infects-himself-with-parasites-for-health-experiment/.

11. Matthew Smith, *Another Person's Poison: A History of Food Allergy* (New York: Columbia University Press, 2015), 180; Mark Jackson, *Allergy: The History of a Modern Malady* (London: Reaktion Books, 2007), 176–77; Nadeau and Barnett, *The End of Food Allergy*, 27.

12. George Du Toit et al., "Randomized Trial of Peanut Consumption in Infants at Risk for Peanut Allergy," *New England Journal of Medicine* 372 (2015): 803–13; David M. Fleischer, Jonathan M. Spergel, Amal H. Assa'ad, and Jacqueline A. Pongracic, "Primary Prevention of Allergic Disease through Nutritional Interventions," *Journal of Allergy and Clinical Immunology in Practice* 1, no. 1 (2013): 29–36, https://www.sciencedirect.com/science/article/abs/pii/S2213219812000141?via%3Dihub.

13. Heather Fraser, *The Peanut Allergy Epidemic: What's Causing It and How to Stop It* (New York: Skyhorse Publishing, 2011); Alex Kasprak, "Are Pharmaceutical Companies Hiding the Presence of Peanut Oil in Vaccines?," Snopes, February 16, 2017, https://www.snopes.com/fact-check/pharmaceutical-companies-peanut-oil-vaccines/. This webpage offers a helpful engagement with Fraser and others who use these arguments to challenge the claims they make. Adjuvant 65 was tested in conjunction with a flu vaccine but ultimately never approved. There were people who received shots containing peanut oil, but the overall number of those individuals is quite small, and those injections happened decades before the increased number of children being diagnosed with peanut allergies. Consult Stacy V. Jones, "Peanut Oil Used in a New Vaccine," *New York Times*, September 19, 1964, https://www.nytimes.com/1964/09/19/archives/peanut-oil-used-in-a-new-vaccine-product-patented-for-merck-said-to.html.

14. Nadeau and Barnett, *The End of Food Allergy*, 28.

15. Dayna Glabau, "Necessary Purity: Western Medicine's Trouble Understanding Allergies Points beyond Simple Explanations of Toxins and Purity," *Real Life*, June 6, 2017, https://reallifemag.com/necessary-purity/.

16. Food and Drug Administration, Palforzia Prescribing Information, accessed August 27, 2022, https://www.fda.gov/media/134838/download; Alison M. Hofmann et al., "Safety of a Peanut Oral Immunotherapy Protocol in Children with Peanut Allergy," *Journal of Allergy and Clinical Immunology* 124, no. 2 (2009): 286–91, 291, e1–6.

17. The patient insert discusses how anaphylaxis occurred at every stage in the effectivity studies. Also, with each step, patients are required to take the new dose in the allergist's office under supervision to determine if an allergic reaction will occur. These doctor visits with specialist copays add to the overall cost of the treatment.

18. Jonathan Gardner, "FDA Approves Aimmune Drug as First Treatment for Peanut Allergy," *Biopharma Dive*, January 31, 2020, https://www.biopharmadive.com/news/aimmune-fda-approval-palforzia-peanut-allergy/571524/; Palforzia website, "Palforzia Pathway," accessed August 27, 2022, http://www.palforziacopay.com/. There is also a patch delivery system that is being tested; perhaps having multiple options might drive down the price.

19. There were two placebo-controlled studies to determine the effectiveness of Palforzia. In 709 Palforzia-treated subjects and 292 placebo-treated subjects, anaphylaxis was reported in 9.4 percent and 3.8 percent of participants, respectively, during the initial up-dosing period. In addition, during the maintenance period of the study, 8.7 percent of participants taking Palforzia compared with 1.7 percent taking the placebo experienced anaphylaxis. (It is unclear why the placebo groups experienced allergic reaction if they were not taking a drug containing peanut protein, unless it was a result of accidental ingestion.) Also, roughly two-thirds of the patients left in the control groups could tolerate the 300 mg dose, compared with only 4 percent of the placebo group. The subjects in both studies were overwhelming

white (78 percent and 79 percent) and male (57 percent and 63 percent). Taken collectively, the studies seem to indicate that this is a treatment that works for two out of three individuals, yet the study populations are not representatively diverse; rather, they reinforce the pattern of making some drugs available only to those with racial, economic, and gender privileges. In 2019, at the FDA approval hearing, concern about effectivity and the risk of anaphylaxis were raised. In addition, there were concerns that the cost would make the treatment inaccessible to many, especially when peanut flour bought at grocery stores is relatively cheap and can be used for similar purposes. One allergist remarked, "They are just packaging up what we already do, in a gold-plated capsule." Once the treatment is made available, it will be important to determine how effective and accessible the prescription drug is for all peanut allergic individuals.

20. The Wikipedia page has this history: "Epinephrine Autoinjector," Wikipedia, most recently updated August 23, 2022, https://en.wikipedia.org/wiki/Epinephrine _autoinjector; Andreas Kanaris Miyashiro, "Mylan's EpiPen Pricing Scandal," Seven Pillars Institute, September 14, 2017, https://sevenpillarsinstitute.org/mylans-epipen -pricing-scandal/; Tracy Seipel, "EpiPen Outrage: Silicon Valley Engineers Figure Real Cost to Make Lifesaving Auto-Injector Two-Pack—About $8," *Mercury News*, October 1, 2016, https://www.mercurynews.com/2016/10/01/epipen-outrage-silicon -valley-engineers-figure-true-cost-to-make-lifesaving-auto-injector-about-10/; and Danya Glabau, "Conflicting Assumptions: The Meaning of Price in the Pharmaceutical Economy," *Science as Culture* 26, no. 4 (2017): 463–64.

21. I am thinking here of the work of Zackie Achmat and the Treatment Action Campaign to make antiretrovirals widely available in South Africa. I am also thinking of pharmaceutical companies in India making generic versions of patented lifesaving drugs available for pennies. There are many interviews with Achmat, and he is featured in multiple documentaries, including *Fire in the Blood* (2013).

22. Christian Hauser, "Epinephrine Injection Kit for Under $10," *Dayton 24/7 Now*, August 25, 2016, https://dayton247now.com/news/local/epinephrine-injection -kit-for-under-10?fbclid=IwAR2iHDZdgWFJNvzxyBECI915lZREjvWYtGioM8kTo7 GNhLfYhJVDgGuhew.

23. I did find one case study of someone using autoinjectors to commit suicide: Cristian Palmiere et al., "A Case of Suicide by Self-Injection of Adrenaline," *Forensic Science, Medicine, and Pathology* 11, no. 3 (2015): 421–26.

24. Danya Glabau, "The Moral Life of Epinephrine in the United States," *Medicine Anthropology Theory* 3, no. 3 (2016): 3, 9.

25. In many articles about Laufer, his lack of medical degree is highlighted. He has graduate training in mathematics, and he teaches mathematics at Menlo College. Mixael S. Laufer, "Introducing the EpiPencil," Four Thieves Vinegar Collective, September 19, 2016, https://fourthievesvinegar.org/?b=001; Charles Piller, "An Anarchist Is Teaching Patients to Make Their Own Medications," *Scientific American*, October 13, 2017, https://www.scientificamerican.com/article/an-anarchist -is-teaching-patients-to-make-their-own-medications/.

26. Jenny McGruther, "Four Thieves Vinegar," Nourished Kitchen, July 19, 2011, https://nourishedkitchen.com/four-thieves-vinegar-recipe/.

27. Four Thieves Vinegar Collective, "Epipencil Autoinjector," accessed August 27, 2022, https://fourthievesvinegar.org/epipencil-autoinjector/.

28. Jackie Farwell, "Disgusted by Soaring Prices, Maine Doctor Devises an Alternative to the EpiPen," *Vital Signs*, March 1, 2017, http://vitalsigns.bangor dailynews.com/2017/03/01/home/disgusted-by-soaring-prices-maine-doctor-devises -an-alternative-to-the-epipen/?_ga=2.234113177.648527547.1577385277-761337650 .1577385277.

29. Scott A. Briggs, "Epinephrine Entrepreneur," *Minnesota Medicine*, May/ June 2017, https://www.mnmed.org/MMA/media/Minnesota-Medicine-Magazine /Feature-Briggs-170506.pdf.

30. Mike Williams, "Rice Students Work Up Wearable to Halt Allergic Reactions," Rice University News and Media Relations, April 18, 2019, https://news .rice.edu/2019/04/18/rice-students-work-up-wearable-to-halt-allergic-reactions/; Justin Tang, correspondence with author, January 21, 2020. There is an existing patent for a bifold option. The EpiWear is a trifold, and Tang and colleagues were told that the similarity to the other device would pose a challenge.

31. Clare Macadam, et al., "What Factors Affect the Carriage of Epinephrine Auto-Injectors by Teenagers?," *Clinical and Translational Allergy* 2, no. 3 (February 2, 2012): 1–7; Shereen Lehman, "People with Allergies Often Leave Life-Saving Epinephrine at Home," Reuters Health, July 2, 2018, https://www .reuters.com/article/us-health-allergies-emergencies/people-with-allergies-often -leave-life-saving-epinephrine-at-home-idUSKBN1JS21E; Christopher M. Warren et al., "Epinephrine Auto-Injector Carriage and Use Practices among US Children, Adolescents, and Adults," *Annals of Allergy, Asthma and Immunology* 121, no. 4 (2018): 479–91; and Jay Portnoy, Rolin L. Wade, and Catherine Kessler, "Patient Carrying Time, Confidence, and Training with Epinephrine Autoinjectors: The RACE Survey," *Journal of Allergy and Clinical Immunology: In Practice* 7, no. 7 (September 1, 2019): 2252–61.

32. Judith Butler, "Rethinking Vulnerability and Resistance," in *Vulnerability in Resistance*, ed. Judith Butler, Zeynep Gambetti, and Leticia Sabsay (Durham, N.C.: Duke University Press, 2016), 12–13; Sherene Razack, *Looking White People in the Eye: Gender, Race, and Culture in Courtrooms and Classrooms* (Toronto: University of Toronto Press, 1998), 138–39; Eunjung Kim, "The Specter of Vulnerability and Disabled Bodies in Protest," in *Disability, Human Rights and the Limits of Humanitarianism*, ed. Michael Gill and Cathy Schlund-Vials (New York: Routledge, 2016), 139.

33. Open Insulin Foundation, "Who We Are," accessed August 27, 2022, https://openinsulin.org/who-we-are/; Dana Smith, "Biohackers with Diabetes are Making Their Own Insulin," *Elemental*, May 30, 2019, https://elemental .medium.com/biohackers-with-diabetes-are-making-their-own-insulin-edbf bea8386d.

34. Here is a helpful look at how the cost, including insulin and test strips, varies by country: T1 International, "2020 T1International Out-of-Pocket Cost Survey," accessed August 14, 2022, https://www.t1international.com/insulin-and-supply-survey/; "American EpiPen Price as Much as Nine Times Higher than in Other Wealthy Countries," *Corporate Crime Reporter*, September 20, 2016, https://www.corporat ecrimereporter.com/news/200/american-epipen-price-as-much-as-nine-times-higher -than-in-other-wealthy-countries/.

35. Bernie Sanders, Instagram Post, December 11, 2019, https://www.instagram .com/p/B58Jgk2hQA7/; Bernie Sanders, Instagram Post, January 9, 2020, https://www .instagram.com/p/B7HSIgYhsxK/.

36. Butler, "Rethinking Vulnerability and Resistance," 19.

37. Katrina J. Allen et al., "Precautionary Labelling of Foods for Allergen Content: Are We Ready for a Global Framework?," *World Allergy Organization Journal* 7, no. 1 (2014): 10.

38. Ann McKeever, "How Restaurant Pros Are Handling the Surge of Food Allergies," Eater, June 19, 2014, https://www.eater.com/2014/6/19/6207199/how -restaurant-pros-are-handling-the-surge-of-food-allergies.

39. Allen et al., "Precautionary Labelling"; U.S. Food and Drug Administration, "Food Allergen Labeling and Consumer Protection Act of 2004 (FALCPA)," accessed March 7, 2022, https://www.fda.gov/food/food-allergensgluten-free -guidance-documents-regulatory-information/food-allergen-labeling-and-consumer -protection-act-2004-falcpa; Beatriz Cabanillas and N. Novak, "Allergic Reactions to Pine Nut: A Review," *Journal of Investigational Allergology and Clinical Immunology* 25, no. 5 (2015): 329–33; and Food Allergy Research and Education, "How FARE Advocates Helped Pass the FASTER Act," accessed August 27, 2022, https://www .foodallergy.org/resources/how-fare-advocates-helped-pass-faster-act.

40. Some Muslims consider all food sources from the ocean to be halal; others consider only fish with scales to be halal. For the latter group of Muslims, shellfish would be considered haram.

41. Sarah Firshein, "Help! I Am Allergic to Apples and Was Kicked Off a Plane," *New York Times*, December 7, 2019, https://www.nytimes.com/2019/12/07/travel /allergies-airplane.html; Rachael D'Amore, "Toronto Woman Says Turkish Airlines Denied Her Boarding Over Nut Allergy," *Global News*, September 24, 2019, https:// globalnews.ca/news/5943853/turkish-airlines-nut-allergy/; Andrew Parker, "Nuts and Dolts: Nut Allergy Sufferer Siblings Told to 'Spend 7½ Hour Flight in Plane Loo' by Emirates Cabin Crew," *The Sun*, April 25, 2018, https://www.thesun.co.uk/news /6144092/nut-allergy-emirates-plane-loo/; and Jen Bowden, "Allergies and Food Intolerances on Flights—How Do Airlines React?," *The Guardian*, April 24, 2017, https://www.theguardian.com/travel/2017/apr/24/nut-allergy-food-intolerance-airline -policy. Some airlines, including JAL and Air France, offer versions of meals without common allergens, but these meals might contain meat products, making them unsuitable for vegans, or might contain substances that are not safe for all (like tomatoes).

42. I appreciate Eunjung Kim for helping me consider a more robust analysis of the allergic calculation, including a focus on temporality and proximity to previous reactions and allergens.

43. Michael Colton, "Peanut Buffer: Allergic Reactions Put the Goober Lobby on the Defensive," *Washington Post*, October 10, 1998, https://www.washingtonpost .com/archive/lifestyle/1998/10/10/peanut-buffer-allergic-reactions-put-the-goober-lobby -on-the-defensive/68dc69a0-6c22-40e3-aa0c-01e4cd6e72a3/; Tess O'Brien, "Food Allergies: Your Right to Be Safe," Food Allergy Research and Education, March 12, 2014, https://www.foodallergy.org/resources/your-right-be-safe-food-allergies-and -law; Roni Caryn Rabin, "Boarding Now: Parents of Children with Food Allergies," *New York Times*, June 19, 2019, https://www.nytimes.com/2019/06/19/health/nut -allergies-airlines.html; and John P. Heimlich, "Status of Air Travel in the USA," Airlines for America, April 13, 2016, https://www.airlines.org/wp-content/uploads /2016/04/2016Survey.pdf. I discuss the links between peanuts and histories of white supremacy in Chapter 2.

44. In the United States of America and Canada, the show is called *The Great British Baking Show*. Season ten is called "collection seven" on Netflix. Chelsea Ritschel, "Great British Bake Off's Rosie Praises Show for Handling of Nut Allergy with 'Nut Runner,'" *Independent*, October 24, 2019, https://www.independent.co.uk /life-style/great-british-bake-off-rosie-nut-allergy-semi-finals-gbbo-catch-up-a9168026 .html.

45. Anita Mannur, *Intimate Eating: Racialized Spaces and Radical Futures* (Durham, N.C.: Duke University Press, 2022), 132, 134, 138–39.

46. The week Henry was eliminated, many overzealous fans took to Twitter to say that Rosie should have been eliminated. They said many hateful things that I will not reproduce here. In a touching exchange between Rosie and Henry, Henry complemented Rosie's baking and said he was "flattered to bake alongside her," while encouraging the various haters to stop tweeting. Rosie replied, "Thank you Henry <3 it's so sad after such a lovely friendly show that people feel the need to be unkind." Harriet Johnson, "Bake Off's Henry Bird Comes to the Defense of Rosie Brandreth-Poynter as Trolls Criticise Her Voice and Looks and Viewers Insist She Should Have Gone Home after Her Pie Exploded," *Daily Mail*, October 16, 2019, https://www.dailymail.co.uk/femail/article-7578837/GBBO-fans -rally-Rosie-Brandreth-Poynter-asks-kindness-online.html.

47. Mannur, *Intimate Eating*, 141, quoting Lauren Berlant's *Cruel Optimism* (Durham, N.C.: Duke University Press, 2011).

48. Rosie Brandreth-Poynter, "Living with a Severe Nut Allergy," Anaphylaxis Campaign, November 20, 2019, https://www.anaphylaxis.org.uk/2019/11/20/living -with-a-severe-nut-allergy-rosie-brandreth-poynter/. The URL is no longer active, but the article can be accessed here: https://rosieandralphbake.co.uk/blog/growing-nut -allergy-article-anaphylaxis-campaign.

49. Brandreth-Poynter, "Living with a Severe Nut Allergy."

50. Glabau, "Necessary Purity."

51. This is to say that it is not a surprise that Rosie Brandreth-Poynter—as a white, heterosexual, cisgendered woman—was the first contestant with food allergies to appear on GBBO. I am also keenly aware of how my own racial and gender privilege means that my nut allergies are often believed and accommodated.

52. Mannur writes, "*GBBO* not just relies on but produces an amnesia of imperialism and resurrects nostalgia for a pastoral English past, a salve against Brexit era England in the construction of this version of an intimate public." Mannur, *Intimate Eating*, 138.

53. The June 19, 2020 (Juneteenth), webinar hosted by FEI was titled "For the Health: A Conversation on Race and Food Allergy." It featured Emily Brown, Denise Woodard (Partake Foods), Javier Evelyn (Alerje), Dr. Lakia Wright-Bello (Thermo Fisher Scientific), and Thomas and Dina Silvera (Elijah-Alavi Foundation). The event was moderated by Linsey Davis (ABC News correspondent) and Karen Palmer (certified professional coach/ operations consultant). A YouTube video of the event is available here: https://www.youtube.com/watch?v=2N-tbNmPhnQ. A follow-up conversation a year later is available here: Food Equality Initiative FEI, "For the Health: Juneteenth Conversation," video, YouTube, June 18, 2021, https://www.youtube.com/watch?v=dYGtpWptahs.

1. Relational Food Allergy, Immunity, and Environments

1. Quoted in Bonnie Y. L. Chow, "'Everybody Else Got to Have This Cookie': The Effects of Food Allergen Labels on the Well-Being of Canadians" (PhD diss., McMaster University, 2011), 79.

2. Susan Wendell, *The Rejected Body: Feminist Philosophical Reflections on Disability* (New York: Routledge, 1996), 145, 151.

3. Marion Nestle, *Food Politics: How the Food Industry Influences Nutrition and Health* (Berkeley: University of California Press, 2007), 1–5, 17.

4. I'm revising this chapter during a period of social distancing and a stay-at-home order from New York State, which means I am keenly aware of how my access to food is being negotiated by limited supply and a desire to avoid exposure to COVID-19. I am eating what I have access to in this moment.

5. Chow, "'Everybody Else Got to Have This Cookie,'" 3, 26; Johan Fischer, "Feeding Secularism: Consuming Halal among the Malays in London," *Diaspora: A Journal of Transnational Studies* 14, no. 2–3 (2005): 275–97.

6. Kamaludeen Mohamed Nasir and Alexius Pereira, "Defensive Dining: Notes on the Public Dining Experiences in Singapore," *Contemporary Islam* 2 (2008): 66, 69.

7. Gabriele Marranci, "Defensive or Offensive Dining?," *Australian Journal of Anthropology* 23, no.1 (April 2012): 90–91, 92–93.

8. Fox News, "Amid Protest, Florida School Stands behind Tough New Peanut Allergy Regulations," March 15, 2011, http://www.foxnews.com/us/2011/03/15/amid-protest-florida-school-stands-tough-new-peanut-allergy-regulations/; Barbara Liston, "Edgewater Elementary School Parents Want Student Home Schooled over Peanut

Allergy," *Huffington Post*, March 22, 2011, http://www.huffingtonpost.com/2011/03/22
/peanut-allergy-edgewater-elementary-school_n_839091.html; and Food Allergy
Research and Education, "Section 504 and Written Management Plans," accessed
August 28, 2022, https://www.foodallergy.org/resources/section-504-and-written
-management-plans. More court rulings are using the language of the ADA to
require educational institutions to accommodate students with food allergies. A
settlement with Lesley University in 2012 set this precedent: U.S. Department of
Justice Civil Rights Division Disability Rights Section, "Questions and Answers
about the Lesley University Agreement and Potential Implications for Individuals
with Food Allergies," January 2013, https://www.ada.gov/q&a_lesley_university.htm.

9. Terry Galloway, Donna Marie Nudd, and Carrie Sandahl, "'Actual Lives' and
the Ethic of Accommodation," in *Community Performance: A Reader*, ed. Petra
Kuppers (New York: Routledge, 2007); Terry Galloway, *Mean Little Deaf Queer*
(Boston: Beacon Press, 2010); and Jose Esteban Muñoz, *Disidentification: Queers of
Color and the Performance of Politics* (Minneapolis: University of Minnesota Press,
1999), 4.

10. Liston, "Edgewater Elementary School Parents"; MyFoxPhilly, "Peanut Allergy
Case Hits Raw Nerve," March 21, 2011, http://www.myfoxphilly.com/dpp/news
/education/032111-peanut-allergy-case-hits-raw-nerve (the threat of contagion is
important to underscore here; kids with food allergies are framed as an inconvenience,
especially when they are assumed to infringe on the "rights" of others); and Matthew
Smith, *Another Person's Poison: A History of Food Allergy* (New York: Columbia
University Press, 2015), 6.

11. Food Allergy Research and Education, "Food Allergy Facts and Statistics
for the U.S.," accessed August 28, 2022, https://www.foodallergy.org/media/1012
/download?attachment; Taylor J. Radke et al., "Restaurant Food Allergy Practices—
Six Selected Sites, United States, 2014," Centers for Disease Control and Prevention,
April 21, 2017, http://dx.doi.org/10.15585/mmwr.mm6615a2.

12. Nicolas A. Christakis, "This Allergies Hysteria Is Just Nuts," *British Medical
Journal* 337, no. a2880 (2008): 1384.

13. *Vital Signs: Crip Culture Talks Back*, dir. Sharon Snyder and David Mitchell
(Chicago: Brace Yourselves Productions, 1995); Michael Kennedy, *My Life in
Institutions and My Way Out* (Altona, Man.: FriesenPress), 27; Kim Q. Hall,
"Toward a Queer Crip Feminist Politics of Food," *philoSOPHIA* 4, no. 2 (2014): 177.

14. Elaine Gerber, "Food Studies and Disability Studies: Introducing A Happy
Marriage," *Disability Studies Quarterly* 27, no. 3 (2007), https://dsq-sds.org/article
/view/19/19; Elaine Gerber, "Ableism and Its Discontents: Food as a Form of Power,
Control, and Resistance among Disabled People Living in US Institutions," *Food
and Foodways* 28, no. 1 (2020): 15.

15. I first wrote these words years before directives were issued to wash hands for
thirty seconds to rid them of coronavirus. Handwashing for others has taken on new
meanings in the age of global pandemics.

16. Galloway, Nudd, and Sandahl, "'Actual Lives' and the Ethic of
Accommodation," 228.

17. McRuer and Mollow cite Ellen Samuels, "My Body, My Closet: Invisible Disability and the Limits of Coming-Out Discourse," *GLQ* 9, no.1–2 (April 2003): 233–55; Robert McRuer and Anna Mollow, "Introduction," in *Sex and Disability*, ed. by Robert McRuer (Durham, N.C.: Duke University Press: 2012), 10–12; Gupta et al., "The Prevalence, Severity, and Distribution," e9.

18. Arizona Food Allergy Alliance, "AFAA's Food Allergy Awareness Week Annual Ad Campaign," 2012, http://www.arizonafoodallergy.org/faaw-wall-photo-campaign .html (note that the Arizona Food Allergy Alliance is no longer active: The Food Allergy & Anaphylaxis Connection Team (FAACT), "Arizona Food Allergy Alliance Passes the Torch to #FAACT," Facebook, August 24, 2016, https://www.facebook.com /FAACTnews/posts/arizona-food-allergy-alliance-passes-the-torch-to-faactthe-arizona -food-allergy-/869878876476323/); Petra Kuppers, *Disability and Contemporary Performance: Bodies on Edge* (New York: Routledge, 2003).

19. Alison Kafer, *Feminist, Queer, Crip* (Bloomington: University of Indiana Press, 2013), 37–38; Robert McRuer, *Crip Theory: Cultural Signs of Queerness and Disability* (New York: New York University Press, 2006); Carrie Sandahl, "Queering the Crip or Cripping the Queer? Intersections of Queer and Crip Identities in Solo Autobiographical Performance," *GLQ* 9, no. 1–2 (2003): 25–56.

20. I am using Alison Kafer's reading of Mel Y. Chen's work to think about my own choices and relationship to bodies and environments.

21. Sami Schalk writes, "I use crip-identified as something different than disability ally because it is an almost-not-quite-yet identification. I am crip-identified not only because my body/mind/desire/behavior is non-normative in terms of race, gender, sexuality, and size, but also because of its precarious relationship to disability as this term is currently culturally understood." Sami Schalk, "Coming to Claim Crip: Disidentification with/in Disability Studies," *Disability Studies Quarterly* 33, no. 2 (2013), http://dsq-sds.org/article/view/3705/3240. I imagine my own corporeality, especially in relation to my allergies, but not exclusively, as not-quite-yet, as in motion, as becoming.

22. Mia Mingus, "Access Intimacy: The Missing Link," *Leaving Evidence* (blog), May 5, 2011, http://leavingevidence.wordpress.com/2011/05/05/access-intimacy-the -missing-link/.

23. Kafer, *Feminist, Queer, Crip*, 12.

24. I appreciate Anita Mannur's suggestions here to think more about the links between smell and bodily responses.

25. Mel Y. Chen, "Toxic Animacies, Inanimate Affections," *GLQ* 17, no. 2–3 (2011): 275, 280.

2. Nut-Free Squirrels and Princesses with Peanut Allergies: Food Allergies, Identity, and Children's Books

1. Mary Rand Hess, *The Day I Met the Nuts* (Earth Day Publishing, 2009).

2. The boy who is allergic to nuts is accompanied by a squirrel throughout the book. The berry-allergic cashier is shown next to a bear, and the boy who is allergic

to bananas is next to a monkey. The animals are represented as being unable to eat foods supposedly integral to their existence.

3. Paul Rabinow, *Essays on the Anthropology of Reason* (Princeton, N.J.: Princeton University Press, 1996), 99.

4. I address this in the Preface and Introduction. There are studies that report, for example, that non-Hispanic Black children have a higher rate of food allergies than their Hispanic and non-Hispanic white counterparts. Consult Kirsten D. Jackson, LaJeana D. Howie, Lara J. Akinbami, "Trends in Allergic Conditions among Children: United States, 1997–2011," *NCHS Data Brief*, no. 121 (Hyattsville, Md.: National Center for Health Statistics, 2013). A more recent study reported that racial disparities in diagnosis and access to treatment continues into adulthood, where nonwhite individuals have higher levels of self-reporting of allergy, with less structural access to treatment and prescription drugs. Gupta et al., "Prevalence and Severity of Food Allergies among US Adults."

5. Stephanie Sorkin, *Nutley: The Nut-Free Squirrel* (Herndon, Va.: Mascot Books, 2013).

6. Two examples are Terry Fox and Norman Malone. Sally Chivers, writing about Fox, remarks that the "quintessential Canadian hero is revered for many reasons and particularly because he appears to be an everyman attempting an exceptional feat. His accomplishment—to run partway across Canada on one prosthetic and one flesh leg—becomes synonymous with what people want to believe are Canadian values of reason, generosity, grit in the face of adversity, and noble independence: in other words, everything Canadians are supposed to want Canada to be" (80). Sally Chivers, "Ordinary People: Reading the TransCanadian Terry Fox," *Canadian Literature*, no. 202 (2009): 80–94. Of course, many people run, walk, hobble, slide, and navigate the world with one foot, two feet, no feet, crutches, canes, wheelchairs, or knees, but Chivers is commenting on how the supercrip trope is reinforced through a nationalism where Fox is assumed to represent "Canadian values" through his inspirational accomplishments. Norman Malone is the subject of the documentary *For the Left Hand*, dir. Leslie Simmer and Gordon Quinn (Chicago: Kartemquin Films, 2021), http://www.normanmalonefilm .com/. When Malone was young, his father hit him in the head with a hammer, leaving the boy's right side paralyzed. Malone learned how to play the piano using only his left hand. At the age of seventy-nine, Malone played Maurice Ravel's *Piano Concerto for the Left Hand* with the West Hartford Symphony Orchestra. Howard Reich, "One-Handed Pianist Norman Malone Makes His Orchestral Debut—at 79," *Chicago Tribune*, October 26, 2016, https://www.chicagotribune .com/entertainment/music/reich/ct-jazz-norman-malone-ent-1026-20161025 -column.html.

7. Eli Clare, *Exile and Pride: Disability, Queerness and Liberation* (Boston: South End Press, 1999), 2–3.

8. Emily Upton, "Apple Pie Isn't Really 'American,'" Today I Found Out, last modified July 11, 2013, http://www.todayifoundout.com/index.php/2013/07/apple-pie

-isnt-really-american/. "Motherhood" was later dropped from the phrase, leaving only the flaky pastry to represent typical Americanness.

9. National Peanut Board, "History of Peanuts and Peanut Butter," accessed August 28, 2022, https://www.nationalpeanutboard.org/peanut-info/history-peanuts-peanut-butter.htm. Commodity checkoff is a program that collects a specified percentage of income from producers to promote products and conduct research. The Got Milk? mustache campaign is a well-known commodity checkoff–funded promotion.

10. Andrew Smith, *Peanuts: The Illustrious History of the Goober Nut* (Champaign: University of Illinois Press, 2007), 12.

11. Smith, *Peanuts*, 15, xv.

12. Leneille Moon, *Patty's Secret: A Tale of a Girl with Food Allergies*, (n.p.: CreateSpace Publishing, 2013). This is one of the very few books about kids' food allergies written by a nonwhite author. As I discuss in the next section, a majority of the texts are written by white authors and feature white boys who are allergic to peanuts.

13. Claudine Crangle, *Woolfred Cannot Eat Dandelions: A Tale of Being True to Your Tummy* (Washington, D.C.: Magination Press, 2015). The author has celiac disease, and although she can eat dandelions, she is "not particularly fond of how they taste." This statement blurs the boundary between biological necessity and preference.

14. Bridget Batson, *Jude the Dude: The Peanut Allergy Kid* (Houston: Bridget Batson, 2007). In the follow-up text, from 2011, Jude hosts a Halloween party for which he bakes a peanut-free cake with his mother. One of his friends, Henry, is allergic to dairy, so he cannot eat the bat-shaped cheese sandwiches. Jude and his mother remove the sandwiches but still serve the cake. Presumably the cake (and the vegetables and dip) are dairy free, although this detail isn't mentioned. Bridget Batson, *Jude Has a Peanut Safe Halloween Party* (Houston: CreateSpace Independent Publishing Platform, 2011).

15. Amber Devore, *My Food Allergies* (n.p.: DNW Publishing, 2014); Kristen Seymour, *No Thank You, I'm Allergic: A Story about Food Allergy Awareness* (Denver: Outskirts Press, 2011).

16. Chen, *Animacies*. Chen discusses how white children are used in public service campaigns about lead in toys—at the expense of addressing the intersections between racism and unsustainable and disabling labor conditions for workers of color: "The image of the vulnerable white child is relentlessly promoted over and against an enduring and blatant background (that is, unacknowledged) condition of labor and of racism: the ongoing exposure of immigrants and people of color to risk that sets them up for conditions of bodily work and residence that dramatize the body burdens that projects of white nationalism can hardly refuse to perceive" (172). "Allergy Facts and Figures," *Asthma and Allergy Foundation of America*, accessed August 28, 2022, https://www.aafa.org/allergy-facts/.

17. Gloria Koster, *The Peanut-Free Café* (Park Ridge, Ill.: Albert Whitman and Company, 2006).

18. Simon does not agree to give up peanut butter in this conversation with the principal. He just argues that Grant is a "cool kid" and states that some students might get to know him if they ate at the peanut-free table.

19. Although the text is not explicit, Simon's limited food options could be understood as a sign of neurodiversity. I appreciate an anonymous reviewer bringing this counterreading to my attention.

20. I recognize the importance of legal remedies when institutions resist accommodations. These remedies have enabled many children to gain access to classroom spaces that were previously closed off to them because of racist, sexist, ableist, or classist policies. Yet the law can only go so far, especially if the institution it is trying to change is itself built on systems of exclusion and domination.

21. Wendy McClure, *The Princess and the Peanut Allergy* (Park Ridge, Ill.: Albert Whitman and Company, 2009).

22. Sue Ganz-Schmitt, *The Princess and the Peanut* (Topanga, Calif.: Wild Indigo, 2011). The peanut is placed eleven mattresses down the from the top mattress.

3. Allergic Reactions through Fluid Exchanges

Chen, "Toxic Animacies, Inanimate Affections," 280.

1. David P. Steensma, "The Kiss of Death: A Severe Allergic Reaction to a Shellfish Induced by a Good-Night Kiss," *Mayo Clinic Proceedings* 78, no. 2 (2003): 222, emphasis added, https://doi.org/10.4065/78.2.221.

2. B. Wüthrich, M. Däscher, and S. Borelli, "Kiss-Induced Allergy to Peanut: Food Allergy Transferred by Love," *Allergy* 56, no. 9 (2001): 913, emphasis added, https://doi.org/10.1034/j.1398-9995.2001.00302.x; Jonathan O'B. Hourihane et al., "An Evaluation of the Sensitivity of Subjects with Peanut Allergy to Very Low Doses of Peanut Protein: A Randomized, Double-Blind, Placebo-Controlled Food Challenge Study," *Journal of Allergy and Clinical Immunology* 100, no. 5 (1997): 596–600, https://doi.org/10.1016/S0091-6749(97)70161-1, quoted in Wüthrich, Däscher, and Borelli, "Kiss-Induced Allergy to Peanut."

3. I pause here to mention of course that kissing was construed as explicitly *not* safe during the COVID-19 pandemic. I am thinking of various public health efforts instructing us what we should be doing in our sexual lives to remain "safe" from COVID exposure. For example, NYC Health cautions, "You are your safest sex partner. Masturbation will not spread COVID-19, especially if you wash your hands (and any sex toys) with soap and water for at least 20 seconds before and after sex." NYC Health, "Safer Sex and COVID-19," October 13, 2021, https://www1.nyc.gov/assets/doh/downloads/pdf/imm/covid-sex-guidance.pdf. The information cautions the reader to avoid kissing anyone not in their "small circle of close contacts," to avoid rimming, to use face masks during sex, to get creative with sexual positions and barriers, and to perhaps incorporate Zoom or text messaging as alternatives to in-person sexual encounters. I mention this briefly to remark on how many of us have recently been making choices balancing risk, safety, pleasure, and spontaneity,

similar to those made by allergic individuals. Depending on our own positionality and ability to access systems of support, we might have more privilege or ability to make certain choices. My work with food-allergic individuals illuminates these discussions. I pick up on these themes in the conclusion to the book.

4. Mingus, "Access Intimacy: The Missing Link."

5. Marcel Danesi, *The History of the Kiss!: The Birth of Popular Culture* (New York: Palgrave Macmillan, 2013), 17–18.

6. Sheril Kirshenbaum, *The Science of Kissing: What Our Lips Are Telling Us* (New York: Grand Central Publishing, 2011), 135–49.

7. Martin, *Flexible Bodies*, 135–42.

8. Tara Meyer, "Warning on Deep Kissing, HIV," *Seattle Times*, July 11, 1997, http://community.seattletimes.nwsource.com/archive/?date=19970711&slug =2548963.

9. Various reasons for not being safe might appear more desirable, including not wanting to prioritize "safety" if it is equated with being boring. Public health discourses of eroticizing safety, especially in relation to sexual activity, might be relevant here to consider how food-allergic individuals can challenge assumptions about safety and quotidian choices. The example from Sloane Miller discussed below attempts to make the discussion of food allergies and kissing less boring or medical. Tim Dean's work on barebacking informs my analysis here. Tim Dean, *Unlimited Intimacy: Reflections on the Subculture of Barebacking* (Chicago: University of Chicago Press, 2009), 24.

10. Kirshenbaum, *The Science of Kissing*, 144–46. Kirshenbaum uses instances of vampirism and of three boys kissing a dead rabid bat as self-illustrative examples of dangerous kissing practices. Positioning allergic reactions next to these examples might do very little to garner sympathy for those who experience the allergic reactions.

11. Hemant Sharma, "Kissing with Severe Food Allergies," *Allergic Living*, April 28, 2014, https://allergicliving.com/experts/kissing-with-severe-food-allergies /; Tess Bantock, *The Ultimate Guidebook for Teens with Food Allergies: Real Advice, Stories, Tips* (Toronto: Food Allergy Canada, 2015), 75.

12. Sloane Miller, *Allergic Girl: Adventures in Living Well with Food Allergies* (Hoboken, N.J.: John Wiley and Sons, 2011), 107.

13. Miller, *Allergic Girl*, 109, 119.

14. Miller, *Allergic Girl*, 112–13.

15. Miller, *Allergic Girl*, 114.

16. One example includes Jaclyn Friedman and Jessica Valenti, *Yes Means Yes! Visions of Female Sexual Power and a World without Rape* (New York: Basic Books, 2008).

17. A. J. Withers, *Disability Politics and Theory* (Halifax, N.S.: Fernwood Publishing, 2012), 118.

18. Mingus, "Access Intimacy: The Missing Link"; Mia Mingus, "Access Intimacy, Interdependence and Disability Justice," *Leaving Evidence* (blog), April 12,

2017, https://leavingevidence.wordpress.com/2017/04/12/access-intimacy
-interdependence-and-disability-justice/.

19. Mingus, "Access Intimacy, Interdependence and Disability Justice."

20. Michael Gill, "A Call for Inclusion?: Human Rights, Intellectual Disability, and a Challenge to Intellectual Superiority," *Psychology Today*, September 6, 2015, https://www.psychologytoday.com/blog/welcoming-intellectual-disability/201509/call -inclusion; Susan Wendell, *The Rejected Body: Feminist Philosophical Reflections on Disability* (New York: Routledge, 1996), 151.

21. Abby L. Wilkerson, "Disability, Sex Radicalism, and Political Agency," *NWSA Journal* 14, no. 3 (2002): 41, https://doi.org/10.1080/09687599.2020.1751077.

22. Lucy Buckland, "Woman with Nut Allergy Has Severe Reaction after Sleeping with Man in First Recorded Case," *Daily Mail Online*, October 10, 2011, http://www.dailymail.co.uk/health/article-2047288/New-fear-nut-allergy-sufferers -First-case-sexually-transmitted-reaction-recorded.html.

23. A. S. Bansal, R. Chee, V. Nagendran, A. Warner, and G. Hayman, "Dangerous Liaison: Sexually Transmitted Allergic Reaction to Brazil Nuts," *Journal of Investigational Allergology and Clinical Immunology* 17, no. 3 (2007): 190.

24. Esther Inglis-Arkell, "Woman Nearly Dies from Allergic Reaction to Sexually-Transmitted Brazil Nuts," *io9* (blog), October 7, 2011, http://io9.gizmodo .com/5846182/woman-nearly-dies-from-allergic-reaction-to-sexually-transmitted -brazil-nuts.

25. Lundy R. McKibbin, Sidney Kin-Hung Siu, Hannah T. Roberts, Michael Shkrum, and Samira Jeimy, "Fatal Anaphylaxis Due to Peanut Exposure from Oral Intercourse," *Allergy, Asthma, and Clinical Immunology* 17, no. 110, 2021.

26. A. Shah and C. Panjabi, "Human Seminal Plasma Allergy: A Review of a Rare Phenomenon," *Clinical and Experimental Allergy* 34, no. 6 (2004): 827, 834–35.

27. Marcos Alcocer, Louise Rundqvist, and Göran Larsson, "Ber e 1 Protein: The Versatile Major Allergen from Brazil Nut Seeds," *Biotechnology Letters* 34, no. 4 (2012): 597–610; Warren E. Leary, "Genetic Engineering of Crops Can Spread Allergies, Study Shows," *New York Times*, March 13, 1996, http://www.nytimes.com /1996/03/14/us/genetic-engineering-of-crops-can-spread-allergies-study-shows.html; and Bansal et al., "Dangerous Liaison," 190. Other theories about the rise in food allergies include C-section deliveries, vaccine preservatives, lack of fetal exposure to peanuts in vitro, and living in urban locations without exposure to dirt and dust.

28. Monica J. Casper and Lisa Jean Moore, *Missing Bodies: The Politics of Visibility* (New York: New York University Press 2009), 109–10, 114, 118–26, 127–28, 130–31.

29. Superfoodly, "It's True: Brazil Nut Selenium & Radiation Poisoning Dangers," November 28, 2016, https://www.superfoodly.com/brazil-nuts-selenium -and-radiation-poisoning-dangers/; Rod Adams, "BBC Bang Goes the Theory Demonstrates That NOT All Brazil Nuts Are Radioactive," *Atomic Insights*, May 4, 2014, https://atomicinsights.com/bbc-bang-goes-theory-changes-mind -brazil-nuts/. There are no examples of Brazil nut proteins being present in other

bodily fluids, such as vaginal fluid, yet because of the indigestibility of the nut, the chance exists that the fluid might contain the allergen. Also, depending on where the nut is grown, the levels of radium in the nut can vary due to the extensive root systems of the trees.

30. Eunjung Kim, *Curative Violence: Rehabilitating Disability, Gender, and Sexuality in Modern Korea* (Durham, N.C.: Duke University Press, 2017), 194, 195; Chris Bell, "I'm Not the Man I Used to Be: Sex, HIV, and Cultural 'Responsibility,'" in *Sex and Disability*, ed. Robert McRuer and Anna Mollow (Durham, N.C.: Duke University Press, 2012), 208–28.

31. Bell, "I'm Not the Man I Used to Be," 226.

32. Paul Farmer, "An Anthropology of Structural Violence," *Current Anthropology* 45, no. 3 (2004): 308.

33. Mingus, "Access Intimacy, Interdependence and Disability Justice."

4. You Ate What? Intentionality, Accidents, and Death

1. "How About a Title for Your First Date" (제목으로 첫 데이트는 어때?), episode 12, *Romance Is a Bonus Book* (로맨스는 별책부록), dir. Lee Jeong-hyo, March 3, 2019.

2. Glabau, "Necessary Purity."

3. "Own Worst Enemy," *This American Life*, transcript, April 13, 2012, https://www.thisamericanlife.org/462/transcript.

4. Sandra Beasley, *Don't Kill the Birthday Girl* (New York: Broadway Books, 2011), 38, 39.

5. The TikTok Benadryl challenge is a social media challenge in which teenagers take large doses of Benadryl to get high. There have been resultant cases requiring emergency treatment, and at least one individual has died from participating in the challenge. Victoria Forster, "Teen Dies After Doing TikTok 'Benadryl Challenge' as Doctors Warn of Dangers," *Forbes*, September 2, 2020, https://www.forbes.com/sites/victoriaforster/2020/09/02/teen-dies-after-doing—tiktok-benadryl-challengeas-doctors-warn-of-dangers/?sh=2bcf3ff8f0db; Dean Johnston and Liam P.A. Johnston, "TikTok Benadryl Challenge: An Alert to Physicians," *BC Medical Journal*, June 18, 2021, https://bcmj.org/blog/tiktok-benadryl-challenge-alert-physicians.

6. Glabau, "Necessary Purity"

7. I recently learned that on the first night of her honeymoon, my grandmother ate strawberries that her new husband bought her even though she was allergic. She wanted to enjoy the berries but suffered throughout the night with hives and a rash. Individuals eat things they "shouldn't" for a variety of reasons, including peer pressure and expectations of social decorum.

8. Website of Tosokchon Samgyetang, accessed August 17, 2022, http://tosokchon.com/sub/sub0203.php?lug=en&mcnt=203.

9. Jong Hwan Jung, Seon-Ho Ahn, and Ju Hung Song, "Minimal Change Disease Associated with Ingestion of Poison Sumac," *Chonnam Medical Journal* 54, no. 3 (2018): 201–2; Dongwon Seo et al., "Development and Method Validation of

Analysis of Urushiol in Sumac and Food Ingredients in Korea," *Journal of AOAC International* 101, no. 3 (2018): 793–97.

10. These are also referred to as the sumac family or cashew family. Ji Hye Kim, Yong Cheol Shin, and Seong-Gyu Ko, "Integrating Traditional Medicine into Modern Inflammatory Diseases Care: Multitargeting by *Rhus verniciflua* Stokes," *Mediators of Inflammation* (2014): 1–17, https://doi.org/10.1155/2014/154561; Han-Seok Choi et al., "Biological Detoxification of Lacquer Tree (*Rhus verniciflua* Stokes) Stem Bark by Mushroom Species," *Food Science and Biotechnology* 16, no. 6 (2007): 935–42.

11. Jina Lyu, "Interesting Korean Food: Otdak Samgyetang (Sumac Chicken Soup)," *Yum Korea*, July 2018, http://yum-korea.com/recipe/interesting-korean-food -otdak-samgyetang-sumac-chicken-soup/ (the URL is no longer active); Jung, Ahn, and Song, "Minimal Change Disease," 201; and "Minimal Change Disease," University of North Carolina School of Medicine: University of North Carolina Kidney Center, accessed September 12, 2022, https://unckidneycenter.org /kidneyhealthlibrary/glomerular-disease/minimal-change-disease/.

12. Jung Eun Kim et al., "Clinical Features of Systemic Contact Dermatitis Due to the Ingestion of Lacquer in the Province of Chungcheongnam-do," *Annals of Dermatology* 24, no. 3 (2012): 319–23, https://doi.org/10.5021/ad.2012.24.3.319.

13. Davey Young, "The Monks Who Spent Years Turning Themselves into Mummies—While Alive," *Atlas Obscura*, October 4, 2016, https://www.atlasobscura .com/articles/sokushinbutsu; Krissy Howard, "The Japanese Monks Who Mummified Themselves While Still Alive," *All That's Interesting*, October 25, 2016, https://allthatsinteresting.com/sokushinbutsu; Alex K. T. Martin, "Eternal Saints: The Art of Self-Preservation," *Japan Times*, accessed August 30, 2022, https://features .japantimes.co.jp/sokushinbutsu/.

14. Heather MacKenzie et al., "Teenagers' Experiences of Living with Food Hypersensitivity: A Qualitative Study," *Pediatric Allergy and Immunology* 21, no. 4 (pt. 1) (June 2010): 600.

15. Margaret Sampson, Anne Munoz-Furlong, and Scott H. Sicherer, "Risk-Taking and Coping Strategies of Adolescents and Young Adults with Food Allergy," *Journal of Allergy and Clinical Immunology* 117, no. 6 (2006): 1440–45; H. Monks et al., "How Do Teenagers Manage Their Food Allergies?," *Clinical and Experimental Allergy: Journal of the British Society for Allergy and Clinical Immunology* 40, no. 10 (2010): 1533–40, https://doi.org/10.1111/j.1365-2222.2010.03586 .x. Both are cited in Tom Marrs and Gideon Lack, "Why Do Few Food-Allergic Adolescents Treat Anaphylaxis with Adrenaline? Reviewing a Pressing Issue," *Pediatric Allergy and Immunology: Official Publication of the European Society of Pediatric Allergy and Immunology* 24, no. 3 (2013): 224, https://doi.org/10.1111/pai .12013.

16. Julie Passanante Elman, *Chronic Youth: Disability, Sexuality, and US Media Cultures of Rehabilitation* (New York: New York University Press, 2014), 132, 135.

17. Lianne Mandelbaum, website of No Nut Traveler, accessed August 30, 2022, http://nonuttraveler.com/; *Allergic Living*, accessed August 30, 2022, https://www.allergicliving.com/; Nadeau and Barnett, *The End of Food Allergy*, 84–85.

18. Mariam Matti, "Natasha Inquest: Coroner Finds Poor Allergy Labeling Led to Teen's Death," *Allergic Living*, September 28, 2018, https://www.allergicliving.com/2018/09/28/natasha-inquest-coroner-finds-inadequate-allergy-labeling-led-to-teens-death/; Jamie Doward, "Pret Allergy Death: Parents Describe Final Moments with Their Daughter," *The Guardian*, September 29, 2018, https://www.theguardian.com/society/2018/sep/29/pret-allergy-death-parents-demand-label-laws.

19. Gina Tsai et al., "Auto-Injector Needle Length May Be Inadequate to Deliver Epinephrine Intramuscularly in Women with Confirmed Food Allergy," *Allergy, Asthma and Clinical Immunology* 10, no. 1 (2014): 39; Susan Waserman et al., "Experts' Viewpoint on: Epinephrine Auto-Injector Needle Length and Dosing Debate," *Allergic Living*, October 19, 2018, https://www.allergicliving.com/2018/10/19/experts-viewpoint-on-epinephrine-auto-injector-needle-length-and-dosing-debate/; Emerade website, "How Long Are the Needles of Emerade, Epipen, and Jext," accessed August 30, 2022 https://www.emerade.com/hcp/faq/needle-length; and Sten Dreborg et al., "Do Epinephrine Auto-Injectors Have an Unsuitable Needle Length in Children and Adolescents at Risk for Anaphylaxis from Food Allergy?," *Allergy, Asthma, and Clinical Immunology: Official Journal of the Canadian Society of Allergy and Clinical Immunology* 12, no. 11 (March 6, 2016), https://doi.org/10.1186/s13223-016-0110-8.

20. Leila Abboud, "Pret A Manger to Label All Ingredients After Allergy Deaths," *Financial Times*, May 1, 2019, https://www.ft.com/content/930f6ea2-6c22-11e9-80c7-60ee53e6681d; Matti, "Natasha Inquest"; Gwen Smith, "Judge Sends Panera Peanut-in-Grilled Cheese Allergy Case to Trial," *Allergic Living*, June 16, 2018. https://www.allergicliving.com/2018/06/16/judge-sends-panera-peanut-in-grilled-cheese-allergy-case-to-trial/. The article mentions that the case was to be argued in front of a jury in 2020. I cannot find any further updates.

21. NFDAR, "About Us," accessed September 12, 2022, https://www.nationalfoodallergydeathregistry.org/about-us; Allergy and Asthma Network, "Online Registry Highlights Personal Stories of People Who Died from Food Allergies," accessed September 12, 2022, https://www.allergyasthmanetwork.org/new-registry-highlights-personal-stories-people-who-died-from-food-allergies/?fbclid=IwAR0qLl-1nXtqUQPAbGbxnoQ9ohE1qaVajbo7qgbZIvpJL04smH_7fQoIeVU.

22. NFDAR, "Anthony L: (DOD: 7/30/2017)," accessed September 12, 2022, https://www.nationalfoodallergydeathregistry.org/anthony-l.

23. Lisa Rutter, "Remembering Those We Have Lost to Food Allergies," *No Nuts Moms Group*, February 7, 2021, https://nonutsmomsgroup.weebly.com/blog/remembering-those-we-have-lost-to-food-allergies; NFDAR, "Cody Hardy (DOD: 11/21/2013)," accessed September 12, 2022, https://www.nationalfoodallergydeathregistry.org/cody-hardy.

24. Mapping Police Violence, "About the Data," accessed September 12, 2022, https://mappingpoliceviolence.org/aboutthedata.

25. Website of Humane Borders, "Migrant Death Mapping," https://humaneborders .org/migrant-death-mapping/; "Our Mission," https://humaneborders.org/our-mission /; and "Arizona Open GIS Initiative for Deceased Migrants," www.humaneborders .info/app/map.asp. All accessed September 12, 2022.

26. Jamie Longazel and Rachel Archer, "The Inadequacy of Prison Food Allergy Policies," *Prison Legal News*, April 15, 2014, https://www.prisonlegalnews.org/news /2014/apr/15/the-inadequacy-of-prison-food-allergy-policies/. For readings on prison abolition, check out Mariame Kaba, *We Do This 'til We Free Us: Abolition Organizing and Transforming Justice* (Chicago: Haymarket Books, 2021) (quote is from p. 24); Angela Davis, *Are Prisons Obsolete?* (New York: Seven Stories Press, 2003); and Andrea Ritchie, *Invisible No More: Police Violence against Black Women and Women of Color* (Boston: Beacon Press, 2017).

27. Longazel and Archer, "The Inadequacy of Prison Food Allergy Policies"; Jennifer Van Evra, "Prison Allergy Death Sparks Investigation," *Allergic Living*, December 3, 2012, https://www.allergicliving.com/2012/12/03/prison-allergy-death -sparks-investigation/.

28. Kafer, *Feminist, Queer, Crip*, 2.

29. Mariam Matti, "Elijah's Law Is Official, Protecting Food Allergy Kids in NY Daycares," *Allergic Living*, September 14, 2019, https://www.allergicliving.com/2019 /09/14/elijahs-law-official-protecting-food-allergy-kids-in-ny-daycares/; Food Allergy Canada, "Sabrina's Law," accessed September 12, 2022, https://foodallergycanada.ca /sabrinas-law/.

Conclusion: Pandemics and the Need for Coalitions

1. Gwen Smith, "DOT Warns American Airlines: Food Allergy Family's Rights Were Violated," *Allergic Living*, June 7, 2019, https://www.allergicliving.com/2019/06 /07/dot-warns-american-airlines-food-allergy-familys-rights-were-violated/.

2. Leah Lakshmi Piepzna-Samarasinha, "Crip fairy godmother," in *Tongue Breaker: Poems and Performance Texts* (Vancouver, B.C.: Arsenal Pulp Press, 2019), 26.

3. Piepzna-Samarasinha, "Crip fairy godmother," 27.

Index

123

Kim, Eunjung, 12, 73–74, 110n42
Kim, Jung Eun, 84
Kirshenbaum, Sheril, 60, 63, 117n10
kissing, 56–57, 59–64, 116n3
Kudlick, Catherine, 74

labeling, 14–15, 28–29, 88–89
Laufer, Michael, 10, 107n25
lead, in toys, 115n16
least restrictive environment (LRE), 35
Leith, Prue, 19, 22–23
Loberg, Kristin, 103n2
Logan, James, 4
London, Cathleen, 11
Longazel, Jamie, 92
Lorde, Audre, x–xii
Luke, Gospel of, 56
Lyu, Kina, 84

Magallanes, Alvin, 22–23
Malone, Norman, 114n6
Mandal, Rahul, 19
Mannur, Anita, 19–20, 22, 111n52
Marranci, Gabriele, 30
Martin, Alex, 85–86
Martin, Emily, 2–3, 61
McMahon, Douglas, 11
McRuer, Robert, 37, 39
Melman, Barbara, 81
migrant deaths, 91
military analogies, 2–3
Miller, Sloane, 15, 64–65, 117n3
Mingus, Mia, 39–40, 58, 67–68, 75
Mollow, Anna, 37
Moore, Lisa Jean, 72
Muñoz, Jose Esteban, 33
Muslims, 30–31, 109n40
My Life in Institutions and My Way Out (Kennedy), 35

Nadeau, Kari, 5–7, 103n2
Nasir, Kamaludeen Mohamed, 30
National Food Death Allergy Registry (NFDAR), 89–90
nationalism, 46, 114n6, 115n16
Nestle, Marion, 27
No Nuts Moms Group, 89–90
No Thank You, I'm Allergic: A Story about Food Allergy Awareness (Seymour), 49
normalcy, 29, 45–46
Nudd, Donna Marie, 36
Nutley: The Nut-Free Squirrel (Sorkin), 45

Obama, Barack, 34
Open Insulin Project, 13
otdak (Korean soup), 83–84, 86

Palforzia, 6–7, 106n19
Palmer, Karen, 24
pandemic, COVID-19, 33, 98–99, 116n3
parasitic worms, 4
Patty's Secret: A Tale of a Girl with Food Allergies (Moon), 47
peanut allergy: air travel and, 17–18; Americanness and, 3–4; as disability, 32–33; drug for, 6–7, 106n19; early peanut exposure and, 5; increase in, 1; kissing and, 56–57, 63–64; vaccines and, 5–6, 106n13
Peanut Allergy Epidemic, The: What's Causing It and How to Stop It (Fraser), 5–6
peanut butter, 45–47
Peanut-Free Café, The (Koster), 51–54
peanuts, history of, 46–47
Pereira, Alexius, 30
Piepzna-Samarasinha, Leah Lakshmi, 98–99
police violence, 90–91
positionality, 58–59, 117n3
Princess and the Peanut Allergy, The (McClure), 53–54
processed foods, 4

Rabinow, Paul, 44
race: food allergy community and, 38; food allergy incidence and, ix, x, 114n4; *Great British Bake Off* and, 19
racism: eugenics and, xii–xiii; food production and, 36; health care and, 99; labor conditions and, 115n16; policing and, 93; segregation and, 34; structural, x, 19, 38, 50
radical access, 66–67
Ray, Tamal, 19, 22
Razack, Sherene, 12
Rejected Body, The (Wendell), 68
representation, ix, 19, 24, 38, 44–46
Richet, Charles, xiii–xiv
risk: communication of, 63–68; safety and, 26–32
Romance Is a Bonus Book (television program), 77–78
Romanello, Marcus, 9

Sabrina's Law, 94–95
safety, risk and, 26–32
Saffioti, Michael, 92–93

MICHAEL GILL is an associate professor of disability studies as well as the disability studies program coordinator in the Department of Cultural Foundations of Education at Syracuse University. He is the author of *Already Doing It: Intellectual Disability and Sexual Agency.*

CPSIA information can be obtained
at www.ICGtesting.com
Printed in the USA
LVHW111824101122
732811LV00003B/462